"Stop What You're Doing and Start Reading"

"Every now and then a motivational/inspirational book comes along that just stands out. My friend Pat Williams has authored such a book, *Who Wants to Be a Champion?* Please stop what you're doing and start reading. And thank me later!"

JOHN C. MAXWELL—*New York Times* Best-Selling Author

"Anyone who desires to climb the ladder of success and become a champion must read and digest this book by Pat Williams. Pat's straight forward approach is right on target."

MIKE DITKA—Former NFL Player and Head Coach

"God thinks you are a champion. Let Pat Williams be your earthly coach. *Who Wants to Be a Champion?* is a must-read for anyone who wants to rise up to his or her highest potential."

KEN BLANCHARD—Coauthor of *The One Minute Manager* and *The Servant Leader*

"Many of us want to be a champion at what we do. However, we have to make it on our own somehow. Pat has taken the time to help put down in writing what works. Now all you have to do is get started and put in the effort to be the champion you want to be."

JOHN TYSON—Chairman and CEO, Tyson Foods

"I appreciate Pat Williams's honest and inspiring words. He challenges every individual to reach his or her full potential."

RICK SANTORUM—United States Senator, Pennsylvania

"Pat Williams takes twenty-five years of examining what it takes to be successful and breaks it down into his ten building blocks of a champion. I recommend this book to everyone who wants to achieve success in all aspects of their lives."
ANDY REID—Head Coach, Philadelphia Eagles

"I've spent much of my life in professional football and national politics learning valuable lessons in life. I have been booed by a stadium of fans, cheered by an arena of political supporters, and ignored by many others. In his new book, Pat Williams shares principles that will help all of us understand the true meaning of success, regardless of whether we are booed, cheered, or ignored. This book deserves the attention of those who desire the best in their lives."
JACK KEMP—Former NFL Quarterback and
Vice Presidential Candidate

"Who doesn't want to be a champion? Pat Williams shows us the huge gap that exists between the desire to win and the desire to *prepare* to win! Champions know the difference!"
DAVID JEREMIAH—Author; Pastor;
President, Turning Point Ministries

"If anyone can help someone become a champion—and a winner in life—it's Pat Williams. This book makes you want to run the best race of your life. Pat's a champ and so is his book!"
KEVIN LEMAN—Author of *Making Children
Mind without Losing Yours*

WHO WANTS
TO BE A
CHAMPION?

FOREWORDS BY GARY CARTER AND GRANT HILL

PAT WILLIAMS

with DAVID WIMBISH

WHO WANTS
TO BE A
CHAMPION?

10 BUILDING BLOCKS TO HELP YOU
BECOME EVERYTHING YOU CAN BE!

HOWARD BOOKS
A DIVISION OF SIMON & SCHUSTER
New York London Toronto Sydney

OUR PURPOSE AT HOWARD BOOKS IS TO:
• *Increase faith* in the hearts of growing Christians
• *Inspire holiness* in the lives of believers
• *Instill hope* in the hearts of struggling people everywhere
BECAUSE HE'S COMING AGAIN!

Published by Howard Books, a division of Simon & Schuster, Inc.
1230 Avenue of the Americas, New York, NY 10020
www.howardpublishing.com

Who Wants to Be a Champion? © 2005 by Pat Williams

Library of Congress Cataloging-in-Publication Data
Williams, Pat, 1940–
    Who wants to be a champion? : 10 building blocks to help you become everything you can be! / Pat Williams with David Wimbish.
        p. cm.
    10 Digit ISBN 1-58229-461-5; 13 Digit ISBN 978-1-58229-461-2
    10 Digit ISBN 1-58229-702-9; 13 Digit ISBN 978-1-58229-702-6
        1. Success—Religious aspects—Christianity. 2. Self-actualization (Psychology)—Religious aspects—Christianity. 3. Conduct of life. 4. Christian life. I. Wimbish, David. II. Title.

BV4598.3.W555 2005
158.1—dc22
                                                                    2005046249
10 9 8 7 6 5 4 3 2

HOWARD colophon is a registered trademark of Simon & Schuster, Inc.

Manufactured in the United States of America

For information regarding special discounts for bulk purchases, please contact: Simon & Schuster Special Sales at 1-800-456-6798 or business@simonandschuster.com.

Edited by Jennifer Stair
Interior design by John Mark Luke Designs
Cover design by The DesignWorks Group, www.thedesignworksgroup.com

This book is dedicated with thanks and appreciation to my friend Bill Glass, the former NFL all-pro, whose prison ministry has touched thousands of lives with the transforming power of Christ's love.

Bill has had a huge impact upon my life and career, especially through his first two books, *Play to Win* and *Expect to Win*. These books helped to shape my philosophy of life, and over the past twenty-five years, I have gone back to them again and again to drink from the wisdom they contain.

These thoughts have fueled my speaking career, and I've studied them in preparation for writing this book.

THANK YOU, BILL, AND GOD BLESS YOU!

Contents

ACKNOWLEDGMENTS

With deep appreciation, I acknowledge the support and guidance of the following people who helped make this book possible:

Special thanks to Bob Vander Weide and John Weisbrod of the Orlando Magic.

I'm grateful to my assistant, Diana Basch, who managed so many of the details that made this book possible.

Hats off to four dependable associates—Andrew Herdliska, my adviser Ken Hussar, Vince Pileggi of the Orlando Magic mail/copy room, and my ace typist, Fran Thomas.

Hearty thanks are also due to Denny Boultinghouse and his fine staff at Howard Publishing and to my partner in writing this book, Dave Wimbish. Thank you all for believing that I had something important to share and for providing the support and the forum to say it.

And finally, special thanks and appreciation go to my wife, Ruth, and to my wonderful and supportive family. They are truly the backbone of my life.

Foreword

by Grant Hill

When I look back over the last four years of my life and all I went through during that time, my biggest regret is that I didn't have Pat Williams's new book *Who Wants to Be a Champion?* to help provide the strength, courage, and inspiration I needed.

As you probably know, I have undergone four major surgeries on the same foot. Because of that, the last four NBA seasons have been stressful and distressing, as I struggled to perform up to my full capabilities.

In addition, my wife, Tamia, has been diagnosed with multiple sclerosis. It seems that we've been struck by one devastating blow after another.

And yet, when I read Pat's book, I discovered that every chapter had words of comfort and inspiration that are applicable to me and, I'm sure, to you, too. Let me give you a few examples.

Building block 1 discusses thinking the right kinds of thoughts. I've discovered that even though I may not be able to choose what happens in my life, I can choose my attitude. And through the darkest times, having a positive and optimistic attitude has made a tremendous difference in my life.

In building block 3, Pat talks about setting goals. And my top goal has always been to come back and play in the NBA at a high level. As I fought to come back from surgery, my goals kept me focused and helped me zero in on what I was trying to accomplish.

Building block 5 discusses the importance of seeking out the right kinds of friends. During my long siege, my friends and family were the greatest encouragers I could have asked for, constantly rooting for me and telling me I could do it. I would not have been able to make it all the way back without them.

Building block 6 talks about taking your hurts and setbacks and turning them into strengths. I have learned a great deal through my adversity—far more, in fact, than when things were going well for me. One day I want to write a book of encouragement and hope for people who have been suffering and show them how they can turn their heartaches into victories.

Building block 8 discusses the importance of refusing to give up, and I also know a lot about this one. There were many times when I had thoughts like, *How can I go on? It's just not worth it.* But I kept pushing myself and refused to surrender, and now I'm reaping the rewards.

Finally, building block 10 is about faith. Through all of my ups and downs, I've always been able to lean on God, and I know that He is my strength. In fact, my main mission in life is not to play NBA basketball—but to please Him.

I know you're going to enjoy this book. Pat Williams writes with clarity, passion, and conviction, and yet he has a warm, easy-to-read style. *Who Wants to Be a Champion?* has been an inspiration to me, and I know it will make a big difference in your life as well.

Read on . . . and then tell others!

FOREWORD

BY GARY CARTER

What a thrill it was to be voted into the Major League Baseball Hall of Fame in 2003. Imagine joining company with the likes of Babe Ruth, Henry Aaron, Willie Mays, and Sandy Koufax!

Yes, I'm terribly proud of what I was able to accomplish during my career as a Major League catcher. I'm proud that I was able to hit 324 home runs, that I threw out hundreds of guys who were trying to steal on me, and that I played for a World Series champion.

Yet more than any of those things, I'm proud because I know how hard I had to work to put up those numbers. I remember all the hours spent refining my skills as a catcher and a hitter. I recall all the times I had to be out on the field—crouching behind home plate—when my knees hurt so bad I could hardly walk.

I still have scars from bone-jarring collisions with base runners. I have on my body the reminders left by dozens of foul tips (and a foul off a 95-mph fastball *really* hurts). I can't even begin to tell you how many times I was clobbered by overeager hitters who didn't stay in the batter's box.

In other words, even though I love the game of baseball, the road to the Hall of Fame was not an easy one. But through it all, I've learned that if you want to be a champion—in baseball or in life—you have to keep going no matter what. You have to keep working when your body is screaming for rest. You have to persevere when the odds seem to be stacked against you. You have to be able to bounce back from failure and be willing to go the extra mile. And most of all, you have to have faith.

My friend Pat Williams (a fellow catcher) also knows what it takes to be a success in life. He knows from personal experience, from years spent watching others succeed and fail, and from many hundreds of hours researching the lives of history's greatest men and women.

In this powerful book, Pat condenses everything he has learned into ten simple building blocks that can help you become the champion God always meant for you to be. I guarantee you, Pat knows what he's talking about. That's why I urge you to read this book carefully and put his words into practice.

I believe that *Who Wants to Be a Champion?* can change your life.

INTRODUCTION

CHAMPIONS ARE MADE, NOT BORN

Before anything else, getting ready is the secret of success.
HENRY FORD

I can tell you exactly where I was the moment I knew I had to write this book. It happened on the boardwalk in Ocean City, New Jersey.

I was in Ocean City for an athletic competition featuring high-school students from across the United States. My son Richie was competing—which, of course, was the main reason I was there—and I was also giving a speech prior to the opening of competition. The event was to be kicked off by a parade of the competing athletes, followed by my speech.

Quite honestly, the parade was pretty disappointing. Most of the athletes didn't seem to have a lot of interest in it. Some slouched down the boardwalk with their shirttails hanging out. They weren't in step with each other. It certainly wasn't anything to write home about.

And then, suddenly and dramatically, things changed.

Marching down the boardwalk, eliciting cheers from the now enthusiastic crowd . . . here came the epitome of precision, spit and polish, and crisp efficiency. These guys were great! Heads high! Chests out! Crisp! Sharp! Every movement had been practiced and polished until it was absolutely perfect.

"Who are these guys?" I asked the man standing next to me.

"They're from a school in Arizona," he answered.

The athletes from Arizona were dressed completely in black. They wore black shorts, black shirts, black socks, and black shoes. As they passed, I saw that each one had something hand-lettered in silver on the back of his shirt. The message stood out against the black background: *Champions Under Construction.*

So *that's* who they were.

I was impressed. So impressed, in fact, that I quickly revamped the speech I was going to give a few minutes later.

It was easy to do, really, because I'd spent more than twenty-five years researching what it takes to build an exemplary life. In fact, I have spent more time preparing to write this book than I've spent preparing to write any other book on any other subject. The speech I gave that day in Ocean City was the foundation of the book you now hold in your hands. This book is the compilation of twenty-five years of research and a lifetime of experience. I have written more than thirty-five other books, and I have worked hard on each of them, but I can tell you that I have never worked harder or prepared better than I have for *Who Wants to Be a Champion?*

I believe that God has put within each of us the capacity to accomplish far greater things than most of us can imagine. He has given each of us the ability to achieve greatness in some special area of life.

I've learned that champions are not necessarily those who were born with special talents, intelligence, or beauty. They are ordinary men and women who achieved success in life because they worked hard to develop the gifts God gave them.

My reason for writing this book is simple: *I want you to succeed in life.*

I want you to succeed because I believe that the success of every individual contributes to the success of the entire world. We human beings are interlinked, and the right kind of success benefits us all!

What's more, I know you *can* succeed. I can say this without knowing anything about you. I don't know your name. I don't know where you live. I don't know where you went to school or what your strengths are. None of that really matters.

You don't have to have an IQ of 140 to be a success in life. You don't have to be a superstudent, a superathlete, or a super anything else. You don't have to be beautiful or handsome. Whoever you are, whatever you do, you *can* be a champion. I guarantee it!

As Charlie "Tremendous" Jones said: "Successful people hate to do the same things that failures hate to do. The difference is that successful people make themselves do what they don't like to do. The failures wait for someone to make them do it."

You may be thinking, *I'm not sure I want to be a champion. I just want to be average.* Well, let me tell you, it is getting harder and harder for the average person to get by in this world. Society is demanding more and more of us all the time.

Another thing I want you to know is that it's not that hard to be a champion. God has put the potential within you, and all you have to do is develop it. It will be well worth it, because champions have more fun in life. They have better careers, happier marriages, stronger friendships, and a sense of purpose that brings them fulfillment and contentment. Champions feel good about who they are and where they're going.

Where are *you* going in life? In the next ten building blocks, I'll tell you how to implement ten building blocks into your life that can help you become a total success—the champion God meant for you to be when He created you.

But before we look at the ten building blocks, I want you to remember two basic characteristics of every champion:

1. CHAMPIONS DREAM BIG DREAMS.

2. CHAMPIONS BUILD A STRONG FOUNDATION.

Let's take a closer look at each of these.

1. CHAMPIONS DREAM BIG DREAMS
Nothing happens unless first a dream.
CARL SANDBURG

Dreams fuel the engine of success. It has been said that what separates successful people from unsuccessful people is the size and scope of their dreams. I believe that is true to a large degree.

But somewhere along the line, we've picked up the idea that dreaming isn't good for us. So we've drained life of opportunities just to sit and think. When a child is daydreaming in class, the teacher snaps at him and tells him to pay attention. We cram our lives so full of activities that the only time we have for dreaming is when we're asleep at night. What a tragedy!

If you go back and examine the lives of the great inventors—Thomas Edison, Henry Ford, Wilbur and Orville Wright—you'll find that most of them were dreamers. They were almost without exception people who were told to pay attention, get with the program, and give up their "foolish" dreams. Can you imagine what the world would have lost if these inventors had listened to their critics?

Here are just a few examples of what dreamers were told:

- Edwin Drake, a pioneer in the oil industry, heard this from drilling company executives in 1859: "Drill for oil? You mean drill into the ground and try to find oil? You're crazy!"

- Western Union president William Orton turned down an opportunity to buy the rights to Alexander Graham Bell's new invention, the telephone, claiming, "What use could this company make of an electric toy?"

- When David Sarnoff, founder of RCA, proposed investing in a new invention called radio, his critics responded, "The wireless music box has no imaginable commercial value. Who would pay for a message sent to nobody in particular?"

- British physicist William Thompson Kelvin, discussing the attempts of some—including Wilbur and Orville Wright—to develop a machine called an aeroplane, heard from naysayers, "Heavier-than-air flying machines are impossible."

I could go on, but I'm sure you get the picture. Things really haven't changed much since the first century, when author Julius Frontinus said, "Inventions reached their limit long ago, and I see no hope for further development." Thank goodness there were dreamers in the world who didn't share that opinion.

What do you dream about? What would you do with your life if God gave you the power to do anything you wanted? How would you like to see your life changed? Your family's lives? What would you do to make your entire community a better place? Is there something you'd like to do to change the world with God's love?

It is not true that all dreamers achieve great things. But I do believe that all great achievers are dreamers. Anyone who wants to become a champion must take the time to dream.

It could be that when I asked you what you dream about, you blushed a little bit because you recognized that your dreams are kind of selfish. Perhaps the first thing you thought about was having a billion dollars in the bank or being a popular professional athlete or movie star. There's really nothing wrong with that. You're only human, and all human beings are at least a little bit selfish.

It's all right to want good things for yourself, but it's also important that you want good things for others too. If you're not dreaming bigger than having a lot of money in the bank, and if your dreams don't include more people than just yourself, you're not dreaming big enough.

Here's something else about champions: they not only dream big dreams, but they also help other people's dreams come true.

I think of Jameer Nelson, now the point guard for the Orlando Magic, whose heroics on the court helped turn a tiny college named St. Joseph's into a basketball powerhouse. During practice prior to the 2003–2004 season, Nelson admired the hard work and hustle of a freshman named Andrew Koefer, who was trying to make the team as a nonscholarship walk-on player.

Despite his efforts, Koefer was about to be cut from the team when Nelson called the coach and asked him to keep the younger player.

"Why?" the coach asked.

"He's a hard worker. He'll help us practice better."

"Is this important to you?"

"Yeah," Nelson answered.

"All right, then."

Koefer made the team.

Michael Bamberger, writing in *Sports Illustrated*, said, "Against La Salle, Koefer entered the game at guard in the final minute and got an assist, his first of the year. On the sideline Nelson was grinning from ear to ear. When Koefer came off the court, the future NBA player said to the walk-on, 'That was a good look, my man.' Asked privately why he had made the call for Koefer, Nelson said, 'A lot of dreams don't come true in life. If you can make somebody's dream come true, you should.'" Amen!

We might say that dreams are the blueprint of future success. They are the architect's sketches of the thing you will build that will one day touch the sky.

2. Champions Build a Strong Foundation

*No one can lay any foundation other than
the one already laid, which is Jesus Christ.*
1 Corinthians 3:11

Before you begin construction on a building, you have to do something that's vitally important: you've got to build a proper foundation.

This concept is aptly illustrated by a story told by my friend, pastor, and author Tony Evans. When a crack appeared in his bedroom wall, Evans hired a contractor to fix it. The man plastered over the crack and repainted the wall, and it looked as good as new. But within a week, the crack was back. The contractor came back out, replastered, and repainted. A few days later the crack had returned. The same thing happened several more times with several different painting contractors.

Then, finally, a contractor told Tony what was really going on. "You don't have a problem with your walls," he said. "The problem is with the foundation of your house. The foundation is shifting, and until it is fixed the cracks will always be a problem."

It's true whether we're talking about buildings or lives. If you want to be a champion in life, you've got to start with a properly built, solid foundation.

Sadly, many people don't want to take the time to lay a proper foundation. They want success, and they want it now. I think that's because we live in a world of instant gratification. We have instant coffee, instant rice, instant mashed potatoes, and one-hour dry cleaning. We send e-mails that travel halfway around the world in a few seconds instead of writing letters that can take days or even weeks to get there. As soon as anything newsworthy happens anywhere in the world, we're watching it in our living rooms, courtesy of CNN, Fox, and the other major television networks. We're not used to waiting for anything! Yet true success doesn't come that easily. It takes time to build a real champion.

So how do you build a strong foundation?

First, *enter into and maintain a proper relationship with God.* God wants to be your friend. He wants it so much that He sent His Son to take the punishment you deserve for all the wrong things you've done. Now, don't think I'm picking on you. The Bible is very clear, in Romans 3:23, that "all have sinned and fall short of the glory of God." The next verse goes on to say that we can be "justified freely by his grace through the redemption that came by Christ Jesus." In other words, Christ came to take the punishment we *all* deserve for the sins we've committed. But you can be assured that if you were the only one who had ever done anything wrong, He still would have come to die for you alone.

All you have to do to enter into a proper relationship with God is to believe in Jesus and accept the fact that He suffered and died on your behalf. As John 3:16 says, "For God so loved the world that he gave his one and only Son, that whoever believes in him shall not perish but have eternal life."

If you're in a proper relationship with God through faith in Christ, all things will be possible to you. If you're not in a proper relationship with God, nothing you do will stand the test of time.

Second, *learn from those who've traveled the road ahead of you.* I read somewhere that in the last ten years, human beings have learned more about the universe than they had learned throughout all the years of history until then. What is more, our learning curve is accelerating as we go along, which means that our knowledge will double again in the next few years. If that's true, it's truly amazing! But it can happen only because of the knowledge of those who lived before us. We are building upon the foundation they laid.

Archimedes, Louis Pasteur, Isaac Newton, Alexander Fleming, Thomas Edison, Leonardo da Vinci, and Benjamin Franklin are just some of the thousands of men and women who have helped to build the world we live in today. In any area of endeavor, it's important to learn from those who have gone before us.

Third, *be willing to work hard.* George and Alec Gallup, founders of the Gallup Poll, spent more than one thousand hours interviewing people whose achievements had earned them a mention in *Who's Who.* All of them felt that success had happened to them because they had worked hard to achieve it. What's more, they all agreed that anyone with a willingness to work hard *can* be a success in life. That includes you.

Fourth, *remember that you're part of a team, so be good to your fellow travelers.* In my opinion, people do not achieve true success in life all by themselves. We get to the top together, helping and being helped by others. The Bible says of teamwork, "Two are better than one, because they have a good return for their work: If one falls down, his friend can help him up. But pity the man who falls and has no one to help him up!" (Ecclesiastes 4:9–10).

Fifth, *develop a desire to improve.* I have known many super-stars during my career in professional sports, and all of them had one common characteristic. They were all determined to do everything they could to get better, no matter how much they had already accomplished.

Larry Bird practiced free throws for hours after leading the Boston Celtics to the NBA title. Mike Schmidt, who hit more than five hundred home runs in his career with the Philadelphia Phillies, took hours of extra batting practice to work on his swing. Kareem Abdul-Jabbar spent countless hours perfecting his sky hook. True champions work hard to make themselves the best they can possibly be.

Finally, *strive to develop good habits.* Some young people think it's okay to drink, smoke, or use drugs when they're in high school and college. They tell themselves, "Now's the time to have fun. I'll get straight later on when it's time to get married and have kids." The problem is that bad habits developed early in life are very, very hard to get rid of later on.

The good news is that it's also very, very hard to get rid of good habits that are developed when we're young. Do the right things now, and they'll become an ingrained part of your personality.

Now that we've poured the foundation of what it means to be a champion, let's start putting those building blocks in place!

THINK THE RIGHT KINDS OF THOUGHTS

As he thinketh in his heart, so is he.
PROVERBS 23:7 KJV

Every action—whether bad or good—begins as a simple thought.

For example, murder is the end result of thoughts of anger or jealousy that were never brought under control. On the other end of the spectrum, selfless service rendered by someone such as Mother Teresa grows out of compassionate thoughts toward the less fortunate.

From these two extreme examples, you can see that it is vitally important to exercise control over your thought life. This is precisely why the apostle Paul wrote, "Whatever is true, whatever is noble, whatever is right, whatever is pure, whatever is lovely, whatever is admirable—if anything is excellent or praiseworthy—think about such things" (Philippians 4:8).

Most of us are so busy that we don't have time to stop and really think about things. We hurry around from here to there in a frenzied rush. Instead of taking control of our thoughts, we let them wander all over the place, wherever they want to go. That can get us into big trouble.

And many of us have gotten out of the habit of thinking. The best time we have for thinking is when we're driving somewhere, but then we usually turn on some music so we don't have to think. If you want to be a champion, you need to find the time to think. Don't drown out your thoughts with music and noise.

What kinds of thoughts do champions think?

1. CHAMPIONS THINK POSITIVE THOUGHTS.

2. CHAMPIONS THINK CORRECT THOUGHTS.

3. CHAMPIONS THINK BIG THOUGHTS.

4. CHAMPIONS THINK PURE THOUGHTS.

5. CHAMPIONS THINK UNIQUE THOUGHTS.

Now let's take a closer look at these five ways of thinking.

1. CHAMPIONS THINK POSITIVE THOUGHTS

The three most important words in the English language are attitude, attitude, and attitude.
SHERWOOD STRODEL

Positive thinking is good for your health.

Literally.

Every time you have a thought, a chemical messenger called a neuropeptide races through your nervous system, depositing tiny traces of chemicals in your cells. If the thoughts you think are fearful, angry, or negative, neuropeptides leave behind chemicals that depress your immune system. If, on the other hand, your thoughts are optimistic, loving, and open, chemicals are deposited that enhance your immune system. In other words, thinking positive thoughts is like immunizing yourself against disease!

My son Alan had a lot of problems when he was in high school. Nothing major. He's a good kid at heart, but he couldn't seem to stay out of trouble. My wife, Ruth, and I told Alan over and over again that he needed to change his way of thinking, to have a more positive outlook. But nothing ever seemed to sink in.

Then one day he came home from school and told his mom about a speech he'd heard. "A man spoke to us today, and guess what he said."

Ruth couldn't guess.

"He said, 'If you think good thoughts, you'll do good things. If you think bad thoughts, you'll do bad things.'"

Ruth fought back the urge to grab him by the lapels and yell, "That's exactly what we've been telling you for years!" Instead, she said calmly, "That speaker was right on."

We're glad Alan was listening this time, and we hope he got the message, because positive thinking really can change a person's life.

Where does your mind go when you're in a pressure situation? Some people can't help but think, *I just know I'm going to blow this.* They believe they're going to strike out when the bases are loaded, roll the bowling ball down the gutter when the game is on the line, or suffer a momentary mental lapse when the calculus teacher surprises them with a pop quiz.

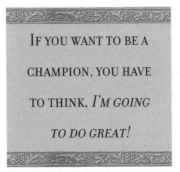

IF YOU WANT TO BE A CHAMPION, YOU HAVE TO THINK, *I'M GOING TO DO GREAT!*

Other people move up a notch and think, *I hope I can do this.* That's better, but it's still not good enough. You've got to do more than grit your teeth, close your eyes, swing at the ball, and hope that things turn out okay.

If you want to be a champion, you have to think, *I'm going to do great!* If you think that way, you'll find that you're right most of the time. Not always, of course, because nobody succeeds all the time, but champions have a positive attitude that helps them win more than their share.

Johnny Mize, who was an outstanding baseball player for the Cardinals, Giants, and Yankees in the 1930s and '40s, once said that he practiced for the next day's game while he was lying in bed at night preparing to go to sleep. "Every night before I went to bed, I'd look in the paper to see who was pitching the next day," he said. "Then I'd lie awake half an hour or so just imagining I was standing at the plate. I'd try to visualize how I might be thrown to, what to look for." No wonder Mize had a career batting average of over .300. No wonder he hit 359 home runs and made it into the Hall of Fame! He kept his thoughts positively focused on the task in front of him.

Even when champions do fall short of the mark, they don't kick themselves for their lack of success. Instead, they learn from their failures and think, *I'll do great next time!*

Champions know that there are many things you can't control. You can't control the weather. You can't control who your parents are. You can't control where you were born or the color of your skin, eyes, or hair. You can't control whether you were born into poverty or luxury. But there is one thing you *can* control, and that is your attitude.

What is your dream? Have your own thoughts been holding you back? If so, unleash them. Let them soar. Most likely, the rest of you will follow.

2. Champions Think Correct Thoughts
*Man's mind once stretched by a new idea
never regains its original dimension.*
Oliver Wendell Holmes

The second way to think like a champion is to think correct thoughts.

Your first reaction to this statement may be, "Impossible. Nobody's right all the time."

True. But I'm not talking about being correct in the same sense that you get the right answer on a math test. Let me explain a few components of correct thinking.

Correct thinking is positive, not negative. I recently had the privilege of interviewing former NFL quarterback Danny Wuerffel on my weekly radio show. Wuerffel is a fine young man who comes from a strong Christian family, and he is also the proud father of a ten-month-old son.

Wuerffel told me that he watched as his mother sat in a rocking chair, holding her grandson on her lap. As she gently rocked the boy, she told him, "You're going to be so smart when you grow up. You're going to be so strong. You'll be a godly man." The child is not even one year old, but his grandmother has already begun instilling a posi-

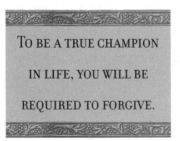

TO BE A TRUE CHAMPION IN LIFE, YOU WILL BE REQUIRED TO FORGIVE.

tive self-image that will serve him well throughout his life.

Danny smiled and told me, "That's the way I was raised." Then he said of his son, "As he gets older, we want him to think of himself as a person who is basically good, even though he may do some things that are wrong. We don't want him to see himself the other way around—as a basically bad person who occasionally does some things that are right."

In other words, they will stress the positive over the negative— and what a tremendous difference that can make in a life!

Correct thinking is constructive, not destructive. Anyone can criticize other people's actions and ideas. It's quite another thing to offer constructive suggestions and improvements to their ideas. Anyone can be a destroyer. It takes skill to be a builder. Some people go around criticizing others for no reason at all. Others never criticize unless it is done in a spirit of helpfulness.

I often pray that God will help me to be constructive, rather than destructive, in every situation and every relationship—and I urge you to do the same. Constructive thinkers focus on improvement. They look for ways to better themselves and their communities. As a result, they make the world a better place.

Correct thinking is discerning, not critical. A closed mind stifles growth and leads to intellectual and emotional death. A mind that is open to every new idea leads to weakness and confusion. Somehow, we have to find a way to be open minded without being gullible and to be discerning without being critical.

The world is full of ideas that can enrich our lives and help us become the people we want to be. But a champion views each new idea in light of what he knows to be true. Any idea that contradicts absolute truth must be discarded.

Correct thinking never holds a grudge. It's not easy to forgive someone who's treated you badly. But to be a true champion in life, you will be required to forgive.

You see, holding on to anger doesn't hurt anyone but you. The person who is the object of your anger probably doesn't even know you feel the way you do. Unresolved anger can lead to all kinds of physical and emotional problems, and, left untended, it can destroy you.

So how do you get rid of anger?

First, and most importantly, *pray about it, asking God to take it from you.*

Second, *make a list of the specific things you're angry about.* Often, merely making a list can help unload those hurt, angry feelings. If a person has done something to hurt you, it can be a good idea to write a letter to that person—even if you know, as you're writing, that you're never going to mail it. The mere act of writing a letter often diffuses anger.

A third thing you can do to get rid of anger is to *review each hurtful situation in your mind,* making the purposeful decision to let it go and never think about it again.

Finally, *you can dissipate anger through physical activity.* You can actually let anger out of your body through whatever physical exercise you choose—chopping wood, picking weeds, pedaling a bicycle, hitting a baseball . . . just about anything.

What do you do if you're angry with yourself? That's a real problem. Some people find it a lot easier to forgive others than to forgive themselves. All I can say is that you have to work at it. Remember that God loves you so much that He sent His only Son to die for you. Ask Him to help you forgive yourself. And every time you find yourself thinking something negative about yourself, switch it to a positive.

For example, instead of thinking, *I really blew it that time*, remind yourself, "I can learn something important from this experience." Instead of thinking, *I hate that I'm so short*, remind yourself, "People tell me I'm fun to be around." Instead of focusing on your weaknesses, focus on your strengths.

Remember that you can't change yourself by worrying and fretting about the way God made you. As Jesus asked, "Who of you by worrying can add a single hour to his life?" (Luke 12:25). So save yourself a lot of unnecessary agony, and just accept yourself the way you are.

3. CHAMPIONS THINK BIG THOUGHTS
Our owner, Arte Moreno, believes that in
order to think big, you'd better act big.
LOS ANGELES ANGELS SPOKESMAN TIM MEAD

What may seem impossible to you today may actually be within your reach tomorrow. But you will never know unless you try. And every attempt to do something begins in your mind as a thought.

I arrived in Atlanta as general manager of the NBA's Hawks in July 1973. During the next three to four months, I met some extraordinary people who believed big and who were on their way to great things in life.

It started when our team chaplain, Wayne Smith, suggested that we invite the governor of Georgia to offer the invocation at our first home game of the season. That's how I first met a fellow by the name of Jimmy Carter. At that time, I had no idea that he would be elected president of the United States just three years later.

Not long after meeting Governor Carter, I had lunch with the owner of the small UHF television station that broadcast Hawks games. He also owned a billboard company, so he was doing all right in life, but he wasn't satisfied. It was clear right from the start that he had big dreams. I'm sure you've heard of him: his name is Ted Turner.

During this time, we were searching for a church home, and someone suggested that we try First Baptist Church of Atlanta. That's where we encountered a dynamic young preacher named Charles Stanley. From the first time we heard him speak, we knew we would make First Baptist our home congregation. Dr. Stanley, as you undoubtedly know, has gone on to be an internationally acclaimed pastor and author.

During this same period, I met two other young men with big dreams.

The first invited me to be interviewed on his television show. I remember that he was broadcasting out of a Quonset hut in the middle of the woods, and the equipment he used wasn't exactly state of the art. If you had told me that Pat Robertson would go on from that humble beginning to have an international television ministry, I probably would have laughed.

The second, a gentleman by the name of Cecil Day, asked me

to give a motivational talk to his employees—a handful of folks who worked for his motel in Atlanta. From that small start, Day built the motel chain that bears his name: Days Inn.

By now, you may be thinking there was something special in Atlanta's water during the 1970s. But it wasn't just Atlanta.

In 1974 I moved to Philadelphia and took over as general manager of the 76ers. On Halloween I got a call from someone who told me he'd just cut a record with a young singer and wanted to know if we'd play it during the game that night. I told him that if he'd bring a tape by the arena, I'd see what I could do.

Before the game, a rather geeky-looking guy stopped by with the tape. I was busy with other matters at the moment, so I pointed him in the direction of the broadcast booth and told him to ask for Joe.

Joe did play the fellow's tape, and even though I thought it was a rather catchy tune, it didn't get a huge reaction from the fans. But a few weeks later, the song "Mandy" was the number one hit in the country, and Barry Manilow, the "geeky" guy who'd asked me to play his tape, was on his way to superstar status.

All of the people I've just mentioned were positive thinkers who knew they were going places in life. They had big dreams and worked hard to make them come true. They did not give in to life-limiting negative thoughts, and they all achieved great success.

It really is true that you don't know what you can do until

you try. Then again, you can't do anything unless you're willing to try. Champions think big thoughts, and they discover that their big thoughts enable them to do big things.

4. CHAMPIONS THINK PURE THOUGHTS
Right thinking paves the way to right behavior.
ANDY STANLEY

Here's a news bulletin for you: God invented pleasure.

He's the one who put taste buds on our tongues and then created things like cherries, oranges, apples, grapes, and strawberries. He's the one who gave us eyes so we could see all the colors in a dazzling sunset, ears to hear music and the sound of rain falling on a roof, and arms so we could have the pleasure of holding those we love.

Our God created pleasure—and that includes the pleasure of sex. Think about that for a moment. He could have made it possible for humans to reproduce in some other way. We could be like some species of fish, for instance, in which the female lays the eggs, and the male comes along later and fertilizes them. But God gave us the gift of sex.

Sex is a wonderful way for a man and a woman to express their love for each other. Sex is also pleasurable without love attached to it. That fact has gotten a lot of people into trouble during the past several thousand years. But when love *is* attached to it, sex is truly amazing.

I know that the human sex drive can be incredibly strong,

and it, too, is a gift from God. So it would be pretty stupid of me to say, "Don't think about sex." But I will say, "Don't think *too much* about sex." In other words, don't let yourself be obsessed with it.

If you want to be a champion, you must respect the opposite sex and keep a tight rein on your fantasy life. And that means you stay away from sexually explicit magazines and movies, pornographic Web sites, strip clubs, and questionable books and television shows.

> A PURE THOUGHT LIFE
>
> IS VITAL FOR
>
> EMOTIONAL, MENTAL,
>
> AND PHYSICAL HEALTH.

It also means that you don't allow your mind to wander into areas where it should not go. Jesus said, "You have heard that it was said, 'Do not commit adultery.' But I tell you that anyone who looks at a woman lustfully has already committed adultery with her in his heart" (Matthew 5:27–28). And one of the Ten Commandments states, "You shall not covet your neighbor's wife" (Exodus 20:17).

Sex, like many other gifts from God, is a wonderful thing when it is used properly—an expression of love between one man and woman who have given themselves to each other in marriage. But used carelessly and improperly, sex destroys lives.

Now I know I've spent a lot of time talking about sex, and that's because a pure thought life in this area is vital for emotional, mental, and physical health. But when I say that champions think pure thoughts, sex is only one of the areas I'm talking about.

First, champions keep their thoughts pure by *refusing to brood over wrong things others have done to them.* We talked about the importance of forgiving and forgetting. Anyone who is consumed by thoughts of revenge is headed for trouble. If you find yourself replaying over and over again in your mind some injustice that was perpetrated against you, make a conscious decision to stop yourself. Don't let yourself go there. Put it out of your mind before it becomes infected and causes you serious trouble. And, by the way, it's important to give other people the benefit of the doubt; don't go around thinking that other folks are out to get you.

Second, champions maintain pure thought lives by *striving for honesty and integrity in everything they do.* Champions aren't interested in cutting corners or trying to see what they can get away with. They achieve their success in life the hard way: they earn it.

Third, champions stay pure by *avoiding jealousy.* Champions avoid comparisons that could lead to bitterness. They don't let themselves get all worked up because a neighbor is putting a swimming pool in his backyard and they can't afford one. They keep their minds focused on the positive instead of the negative. Jealousy, left unchecked, can become a fast-growing cancer that can consume you.

Finally, champions cultivate pure thoughts by *staying away from drugs and alcohol.* We'll talk more about these mind-altering substances later on. But for now, I'll just say that champions avoid substances that can impair their thinking, cloud their judgment, and cause them to be less than their best.

5. CHAMPIONS THINK UNIQUE THOUGHTS

Superstars don't think like everyone else. They eliminate worry, envy, jealousy, embarrassment, and anger. The superstar thinks a lot less and holds a thought longer.
JIM FANNIN

Champions are willing to think outside the box. They don't feel that they have to go along with the crowd on everything. They're willing to be themselves no matter what anyone else thinks or does.

It's only because champions were willing to think outside the box that we now have things like automobiles, airplanes, television, electric lights, personal computers, telephones, cell phones, movies, CDs and DVDs, and immunizations against diseases.

I recently read about a college psychology class where the professor showed his class how peer pressure works. He asked ten students to leave the room. He then held up a red paper square and asked the rest of his students to agree that it was green.

When the ten students who had been asked to wait outside were readmitted to the classroom, the professor again held up the red square. "Raise your hand if you see a green square," he said. Almost everyone raised their hands, including six of the ten students who had left the classroom.

"That," the professor declared, "is peer pressure. The power of group dynamics can get the individual to do just about anything."

If you want to be a champion, you'll be willing to say, "That's red," even if everyone else says, "It's green."

It's okay to stand out from the crowd, because the crowd is not always right. Jesus warned us about the dangers of going along with the crowd. He said, "Wide is the gate and broad is the road that leads to destruction, and many enter through it. But small is the gate and narrow the road that leads to life, and only a few find it" (Matthew 7:13–14).

I had dinner with my son David in California. He told me this story about his time as a marine at the start of the invasion of Iraq in March 2003:

> It was tough duty, and a lot of soldiers were scared and didn't want to be there. Some had bad attitudes, including the officers. Dad, I remember all the times you told us about the importance of having a good attitude. I'd get up in the morning and say, "It's a good day today, and we're going to go get 'em." Stuff like that. Some of the officers said, "Are you all right, soldier? Are you suicidal?" I didn't want to be there, and I was fearful, but my behavior was based on my attitude. I'd say, "We're on the right side. We're going to win this thing!" Pretty soon I saw most of the other soldiers, including some of the officers, begin to come

around. I'm convinced my attitude had a lot to do with it. Attitude is everything in life.

Learn to think for yourself. Be willing to walk on down the road alone if you have to. It may seem lonely right now, but in the long run you'll be a blessing not only to yourself but also to others.

BUILDING BLOCK

SAY THE RIGHT KINDS OF WORDS

Wise men talk because they have something to say;
fools, because they have to say something.
PLATO

More than any other way, people will judge you by the words you speak. If you choose your words carefully and speak articulately, people will see you as intelligent and competent. But if you're careless in your grammar and use words incorrectly, you'll be viewed as someone who's not exactly the brightest light bulb in the house.

If you speak clearly and confidently, people will say, "Now, there's somebody to be reckoned with." But if you tend to mumble or slur your words, they are likely to think that you're a pushover. Fair or not, that's the way it is.

The plain truth is that the person who speaks clearly, articulately, and confidently is much more likely to become a champion in his or her chosen field of endeavor.

The good news is that almost anyone can learn to speak clearly and confidently. It just takes practice. And there are lots of ways to practice! You can read books on effective oral communication. You can rehearse in front of a mirror. You can join an organization like Toastmasters, where you have to give impromptu speeches on a regular basis. And you can improve your communication by adding to your vocabulary. I believe reading is the best way to do this. Through reading, you will not only learn new words, but you will also see the context in which they are used.

I'm not suggesting that you sprinkle your speech with six-syllable words. Anybody who does that will merely sound pre-tentious. But having an expansive vocabulary so that you can use the right words at the right moment can only help you.

WORDS CAN ENCOURAGE AND INSPIRE GREATNESS, AND THEY CAN TEAR DOWN AND DESTROY.

While I'm on the subject of vocabulary, let me say something about slang. Every generation has its own "street language." Way back when I was a kid, the cool people called each other "daddio" or "real gone cats," and they got a kick out of saying "later" for "good-bye." I can give you a long list of words that have meant something was really great: *cherry, neat, keen, boss, groovy, fab, gear, far-out, out of sight, killer,* and *sweet.* And those are just off the top of my head. It's not necessarily wrong to use slang, but it's important to be careful about using it at the wrong time. It may be fine to be cool when you're with friends who speak the same language, but it's not so fine when you're speaking to a potential employer.

In my long career I have had the strange experience of interviewing some job applicants who left me wondering what they were talking about! I felt like I needed an interpreter. I'm sure they were really cool or groovy or boss or whatever the word was at the moment—but they didn't get the job.

Timing is everything! It's important to know how to speak the right words at the right moment.

Words have enormous power. They can give life, and they can bring death. They can encourage and inspire greatness, and they can tear down and destroy. The book of James says that the tongue "corrupts the whole person, sets the whole course of his life on fire, and is itself set on fire by hell" (James 3:6).

And Jesus said, "I tell you that men will have to give account on the day of judgment for every careless word they have spoken. For by your words you will be acquitted, and by your words you will be condemned" (Matthew 12:36–37).

If you want to be a champion, it is vitally important that you learn to use positive words of truth, health, and life.

Here are some important things to remember about the words you use:

1. SPEAK WORDS THAT ARE POSITIVE.

2. STRIVE TO SPEAK THE TRUTH IN LOVE.

3. LISTENING IS MORE IMPORTANT THAN SPEAKING.

4. DON'T BE AFRAID TO ASK QUESTIONS.

5. PROFANITY IS NEVER NECESSARY.

1. SPEAK WORDS THAT ARE POSITIVE

*I can live for two months
on one good compliment.*
MARK TWAIN

When my children were young, I challenged them to a ninety-day test. During that period, they were to speak only positive, encouraging, uplifting, and kind words. If anything negative or discouraging came out of their mouths, they had to start over—and believe me, there was plenty of starting over. But I knew that if they spoke only positive words for ninety days, they'd never want to go back to their old way of behavior.

Today, I want to issue you the same challenge. If you will strive to speak only positive words for ninety days, every relationship you have will be radically transformed. Your life will change dramatically for the better. Try it and see!

People who try to be positive are fun to be around and generally have a lot of friends. On the other hand, everyone tries to avoid people who constantly criticize and complain. I believe there is a spiritual law at work here. In general, negative talk brings about negative consequences. People tend to live up, or down, to the words they speak.

I understand that to some degree, the way we look at life depends on the personality we were born with. Some people tend to be optimistic about everything, and I admit that I'm one of them. But you know what? For the most part, being positive and optimistic has worked for me. I believe good things are going to happen, and they do! This doesn't mean my life has been trouble free. Not by a long shot! But through it all, I've tried to look on the bright side of everything, and I feel that God has blessed me because of it.

It could be that you have a natural tendency to see the dark cloud behind every silver lining. If that is true, then you need to make a serious effort to change the things you say. When you find yourself about to say something negative or critical, quit talking. As Will Rogers said, "Never miss a good chance to shut up." And then try to think of something positive to say. Force yourself to notice the good in every person and every situation, and use your words to encourage others.

When my son Bobby attended Edgewater High School in Orlando, he was the catcher for the baseball team. Naturally, I was proud to see him following in my footsteps. I was also a catcher in high school, college, and for a couple of years in the Phillies organization. One day, I was particularly proud of Bobby because he had a great game. He had two hits, threw out a runner trying to steal second, blocked the plate and tagged out another runner trying to score, and stopped several pitches thrown into the dirt.

On the way home after the game, I asked Bobby what he would remember most about the experience. He answered without hesitation, "Coach Barton shook my hand and told me I did a good job."

Such is the importance of encouragement.

Everyone needs to be congratulated after a job well done. But I think it is even more important to receive words of encouragement after you stumble in some way. Nobody needs to hear "You blew it" when they've messed up. They already know things didn't work out the way they wanted; they don't need any reminders. What they do need is for someone to say, "That was a nice try" or, "Hang in there—you'll get 'em next time."

One thing that makes champions so successful in life is that they are encouragers. And because they are encouragers, they are good motivators, able to get the very best out of other people. Thus, they lift the entire group to a higher level.

Champions speak positive words, and they encourage others to do their very best.

2. STRIVE TO SPEAK THE TRUTH IN LOVE

*Speaking the truth in love, we will in all things grow up
into him who is the Head, that is, Christ.*

EPHESIANS 4:15

Have you ever known anybody who was so honest that if he or
she called you on the Fourth of July and told you it was snow-
ing, you'd put on your boots before you went outside?

I have, so I know how great it can be to have a friend you
can count on to tell you the truth at all times.

Champions are noted for their honesty. If they tell you
something, you can take it to the bank. Their honesty makes
them indispensable to the success of businesses and other or-
ganizations. Truthfulness is just one of the qualities that propels
them forward on the road to success in life.

During the past couple of years, a number of American
businesses have come crashing down—Enron and WorldCom
the most notable examples—because they had built their success on a foundation of lies. There were not enough people willing to tell the truth at all times despite any cost involved, and
the result was a shameful, expensive disaster.

In a recent study, twenty-six hundred top-level managers
were asked to list the characteristics they looked for in a leader.
The landslide winner was honesty. It finished ahead of intelligence, competency, and being inspirational.

If you want to have a successful career—in business or in
any other endeavor—then tell the truth.

Jesus said that the devil is "a liar and the father of lies" (John 8:44). Obviously, then, someone who consistently tells lies is on the wrong side of the battle between good and evil. Champions are those who strive to tell the truth in all situations, even when it puts them in an uncomfortable position or causes discomfort to someone they care about.

Yet champions always attempt to tell the truth in a spirit of kindness and love. If your friend is trying on a new dress and asks you how she looks in it, it might be truthful to say, "Like the big loser in a paintball battle, that's how. It's horrible." But it certainly wouldn't be kind. It would be far better to say something like, "I just don't think that color is right for you."

In a situation like this, it's important to question your motives. Are you getting some personal satisfaction out of telling a truth that hurts someone's feelings? Or are you telling the truth simply because it *is* the truth, and everyone has a right to know the truth?

The "new dress" example is a very simple one, I know. There are many other situations where it's much tougher to tell the truth. But in all of them, the need to speak the truth goes hand in hand with the need to be loving and kind to others.

3. LISTENING IS MORE IMPORTANT THAN SPEAKING

I like to listen. I have learned a great deal from listening carefully.
ERNEST HEMINGWAY

God knows how important it is to listen. That's why He gave us two ears and only one mouth! I've never heard an employee say about his boss, "I just wish he'd stop listening so much." I've never heard anyone say, "If we'd all just stop listening to each other, we might get something done around here!" Listening is one of the most important things you can do.

Champions make it a point to listen to other people. They don't just pretend to listen; they really listen. They understand that you can't learn if you don't listen—that you can't really get to know people if you don't listen to what they have to say.

This is the age of information. There are all kinds of important truths to be heard. But we can't hear them if we're always talking instead of listening. Socrates once told a disciple, "Speak, young man, that I may know you." Today, we turn that around to, "Be quiet, young man. I want to tell you about myself." Recently, comedienne Caroline Rhea said, "Being in therapy is great. I spend an hour just talking about myself. It is kinda like being the guy on a date."

Sadly, I'm convinced that most people don't know how to listen. While other people are talking, we're thinking about what we're going to say in reply or daydreaming about something completely unrelated. Even worse, sometimes we're wishing the other person would hurry up and finish what he's saying so we can talk about ourselves.

I find that, in general, parents don't listen to their children, children don't listen to their parents, wives don't listen to their husbands, husbands don't listen to their wives, and friends don't listen to their friends. If you were to interview people as they came out of a Sunday morning church service and ask them to tell you what the sermon was about, I'd bet that most wouldn't know. Why not? Because they weren't really listening.

Instead, Dad was thinking about the problems waiting for him at work on Monday morning. Mom was thinking about that conference she had with her child's teacher on Friday. And the kids were thinking about what they were going to do when they got home from church.

Jesus had a lot to say about the importance of listening. He said, "He who has ears, let him hear" (Matthew 11:15). And He had harsh words for people who weren't really listening to the truths He was trying to get across to them: "Though seeing, they do not see; though hearing, they do not hear or understand" (Matthew 13:13). Jesus could just as well have been talking to Americans today. People's social skills haven't improved much during the last several centuries.

A champion understands how important listening is to the art of conversation—and friendship.

Some of us have trouble listening to other people because we're in too much of a hurry. I am by nature a high-energy individual, which means that I've had to learn how to listen patiently. This is especially true where my nineteen children are concerned (fourteen of whom are adopted from countries where English is not the primary language). When they were younger, some of my kids took a very long time to get to the "punch line" of what they were trying to tell me. Often, I found my mind wandering, and I had to purposefully bring it back to the present. Other times, I had to fight off the urge to look or act impatient.

I have discovered that some people get right to the point. They tell things quickly, clearly, and in an interesting way. Other people tend to meander here and there before they finally get to their destination. Either way, an effective listener gives people time to say what they need to say. He or she doesn't rush them by looking or acting impatient. He doesn't steal not-so-subtle glances at his watch. He doesn't look off into space or roll his eyes. One of the best courtesies a champion can show other people is to listen, with interest, to whatever they have to say.

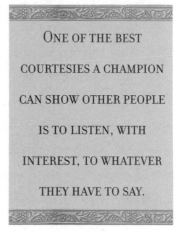

ONE OF THE BEST COURTESIES A CHAMPION CAN SHOW OTHER PEOPLE IS TO LISTEN, WITH INTEREST, TO WHATEVER THEY HAVE TO SAY.

Please forgive me if you think I am stereotyping, but experience tells me that most women like to tell things in "prose style." In other words, a woman will start off an account of something important that happened to her by saying something like, "You'll never guess what happened to me today!" Then she will rewind back to the very beginning of the day's adventure, unfolding all the details as a novelist would do, gradually building up to the exciting climax of the story.

Most men, on the other hand, tell things in "news style." They use a format every newspaper reporter knows as "the inverted pyramid." In the inverted pyramid, you start off by telling the most important thing—as in a news bulletin—and then add other details in descending order of importance. Instead of starting off with, "You'll never guess what happened to me today," a man is likely to say, "I got a big promotion today!" Then he'll tell what he was promoted to, how much of a raise he got, who delivered the happy news, and so on.

This difference of styles leads to some difficulties in marriages. Wives claim their husbands don't listen to them; husbands say their wives take too long to get to the point. Wives say their husbands don't keep them properly informed about what's going on in their lives; husbands say they give plenty of information, but their wives seem to want more.

The bottom line is that it's vitally important to learn to be accepting of other people's styles of communication and to listen accordingly.

4. DON'T BE AFRAID TO ASK QUESTIONS
It is better to look uninformed than to be uninformed.
Curb your ego and keep asking questions.
RICHARD THALHEIMER

Ask any woman to tell you what men do that annoy her, and one of the answers bound to show up on her top-ten list is: "They never stop and ask for directions when they're lost."

I'll agree with that. Men aren't so good when it comes to admitting that they don't know where they are or what they're doing. For example, if a man doesn't know anything about cars, he'll never admit it to his mechanic. The mechanic may say something like, "The ringmaster hydriculater has a hyperbolated sprocket joint in the apex converter." The mechanically impaired guy will nod in a knowing way and respond, "That's just what I thought."

Although females are usually better than males when it comes to admitting their ignorance about some matter, I do believe that fear of asking questions is common to both sexes. Most people hate to admit that they don't know something. It makes us feel as if we're not as smart as the next person. Actually, though, we all have our areas of expertise and our areas of ignorance.

If you asked the right questions, you could learn something important from just about everybody you know. And, conversely, if everybody you know asked you the right questions, they could learn something from you. But if you don't ask questions, it's unlikely that you'll ever gain knowledge in those areas where your own experience or education is lacking.

Champions ask questions. They have an insatiable curiosity. According to business expert Warren Bennis, "Effective executives, no matter how high they rise, remain inquisitive; curious about everything. They read, go around, look, explore, wonder, make connections, always know that their company is not a whole, but only part of it. They are, by nature, restless, never satisfied, ever aware that there is no such thing as perfection, convinced that any product can be improved and any procedure upgraded."

What are you curious about? Start asking questions!

5. PROFANITY IS NEVER NECESSARY
I find it distressing to witness the way filth and sacrilege have infiltrated our speech in Western nations.
DR. JAMES DOBSON

Can anybody tell me why cursing and swearing have become so prevalent these days? I hear profanity everywhere, and I hate it! To me, a foul mouth is a demonstration of a lack of intelligence. When I hear people sprinkle their speech with profanity, I just assume they have a very limited vocabulary. Otherwise it wouldn't be necessary to resort to profanity.

You hear a lot of talk about secondhand smoke these days. I believe cigarette smoke is dangerous, and I'm grateful for laws that protect nonsmokers from its effects. And though I realize that profanity is not as deadly as tobacco smoke, I feel that people who use it are polluting the air in much the same way smokers do. Profanity is an unwelcome invasion of my air space. It is degrading and disgusting, and I shouldn't have to hear it. I believe that people who curse and swear in public have no sense of courtesy or respect for others.

Ulysses S. Grant, who served as the Union's top general during the Civil War and as America's president after the war, was known as a man who never used profanity. When asked why not, he replied:

> I never learned to swear. When a boy, I seemed to have an aversion to it, and when I became a man, I saw the folly of it. I have always noticed, too, that swearing helps to rouse a man's anger, and when a man flies into a passion, his adversary who keeps cool always gets the better of him. In fact, I could never see the use of swearing. I think it is the case with many people who swear excessively that it is a mere habit, and that they do not mean to be profane, but, to say the least, it is a great waste of time.

Grant's words are as valid today as they were more than one hundred years ago. Profanity does not benefit the person who uses it, so why use it at all?

It would be impossible for me to overstate the importance of using the right words. Words can build, and they can destroy. They can bring life, and they can kill.

As every champion knows, the ability to use words wisely will carry you far in life.

SET SPECIFIC GOALS

*Without a goal, we are much like the man
with a boat and nowhere to go.*
EARL NIGHTINGALE

It happened during the Olympic Games in Athens during the summer of 2004.

American sharpshooter Matt Emmons was well on his way to a gold medal in the 50-meter rifle competition. He was so far out in front there didn't seem to be even a remote possibility that anyone could catch him. He'd have to blow it big-time for that to happen, and that wasn't likely.

Matt peered through the scope . . . aimed carefully . . . tightened his finger on the trigger: *blam!*

Bull's-eye! Matt had won the gold!

But wait a minute. What were the judges shouting about?

Somehow, Matt Emons had become confused. He was shooting at the wrong target!

You don't get points for hitting the wrong target—even if

you do hit it right in the center—and Emmons fell to an eighth-place finish, far out of the running for a medal.

Of course, this was a devastating loss for Matt, although he handled it like the fine, young Christian man he is. But the rest of us can learn something very important from Matt's mix-up. That is, everyone must have a target to aim for in life, and it must be the right one!

My friend Tony Evans had a similar experience: "While in seminary I learned a very valuable lesson in one of my classes, but not from a textbook or a lecture. One of my professors required an extensive research paper, and I really wanted to produce an A-plus paper. I did the research, pulled all-nighters, and wrote extra pages. When I received my graded paper from the professor, there was an F at the top. I was crushed. The professor wrote a little note: 'Great scholarship, great detail, magnificent effort, but you answered the wrong question.'"

IF YOU LAUNCH OUT INTO LIFE NOT KNOWING WHAT YOUR GOALS ARE, HOW CAN YOU POSSIBLY SUCCEED?

Not long ago, I spoke to a group of about twenty teenagers. Before I began to speak, I went around the room and asked them all to tell me their names, ages, where they went to school, and what they'd like to be doing ten years from now.

They all knew their names, ages, and where they went to school—which pleased me—but only two of them had the slightest idea what they wanted to be doing in a decade. Most of them said things like, "I want to be happy" or "I want to be rich." Another favorite was, "I want to be married."

They didn't have specific goals—only general wishes.

If you launch out into life not knowing what your goals are, how can you possibly succeed? My answer: you can't!

I was seven years old when my dad took me to my first Major League baseball game at old Shibe Park at the corner of Twenty-first and Lehigh in Philadelphia. The date was June 15, 1947, and we went to a doubleheader between the Philadelphia A's (who have since called both Kansas City and Oakland home) and the Cleveland Indians.

I remember that the A's and Indians split the two games— and I also remember that before we left the park that day, I knew my life's goal: I wanted to be a Major League Baseball player. I loved every moment my dad and I spent together at the ballpark that afternoon. I was mesmerized by the sights, sounds, and smells of baseball.

Shortly after that, my dad gave me my first baseball glove—a catcher's mitt—and I dedicated myself to learning how to stop wild pitches, throw out would-be base stealers, and block home plate to keep runners from scoring on throws from the outfield.

No, I never did make it to the major leagues. But I played baseball in high school, college, and for a couple of years in the minor leagues. And it was my experiences in baseball that opened the door to my successful and gratifying career in professional sports—a career that has now spanned more than forty years. I know, beyond a doubt, that my life changed because of that visit to Philadelphia's Shibe Park on a warm spring day more than fifty-five years ago.

Where are you headed in life? Have you thought about the specific steps you'll need to take to get there? Have you figured out how long it will take you? That's what goals are all about.

We've already seen the importance of dreaming big dreams. Goal setting is the nuts and bolts of turning those dreams into reality.

The apostle Paul knew all about the importance of setting goals. He wrote: "I press on to take hold of that for which Christ Jesus took hold of me. Brothers, I do not consider myself yet to have taken hold of it. But one thing I do: Forgetting what is behind and straining toward what is ahead, I press on toward the goal to win the prize for which God has called me heavenward in Christ Jesus" (Philippians 3:12–14).

God's people are always on the move, pressing forward to victory. They set goals that are consistent with God's will for their lives, and then they persevere in the direction of those goals. Or, as Paul wrote, they "press on."

Here's another thing the apostle Paul said about goals: "We make it our goal to please him [God]" (2 Corinthians 5:9). Living a life that is pleasing to God should be everyone's number one goal. As a Christian, I do everything I can to make sure that the goals I set for myself are consistent with God's plan for my life.

To help you get where you want to be:

1. GOALS MUST BE REALISTIC.

2. GOALS MUST BE WRITTEN DOWN.

3. GOALS MUST BE SPECIFIC ENOUGH TO MEASURE.

4. GOALS MUST HAVE A DEADLINE.

5. GOALS MUST BE BROKEN INTO SHORT-TERM AND LONG-TERM GOALS.

1. GOALS MUST BE REALISTIC

If you're climbing the ladder of life, you go rung by rung, one step at a time. Don't look too far up. Set your goals high, but take one step at a time.
DONNY OSMOND

What do I mean when I say your goals should be realistic? I can best explain by telling you about a couple of moms whose sons were both first-semester freshmen at a prestigious university.

One proud mother said to the other, "My Ralph is going to be a brain surgeon. Or an astronaut. And in his leisure time, he plans to be a conductor for a symphony orchestra. What about your son, Walter? What are his plans?"

Walter's mother smiled and said simply, "Right now, he's just hoping that he becomes a sophomore."

The second mother understood the importance of setting realistic goals.

Now, I don't mean to say that a goal should be easy to obtain. If there's no challenge involved, then there's no need to set a goal in the first place. But neither should a goal be so far out of your reach that it's like trying to climb your way to the moon. Ralph is never going to be a brain surgeon if he doesn't first become a sophomore.

Hal Urban says that some people confuse goals with wishes. "A wish is a vague dream that we hope happens to us," he says. "A goal is a clear picture which becomes an achievement because we make it happen. It requires hard work, self-discipline, and good use of time." He goes on to say, "We draw up plans for buildings, businesses, meetings, weddings, sports, parties, vacations, retirement, etc., but do we draw up plans for our lives? That's what goals are. One of the best investments you'll ever make is to invest some time in sitting down, thinking, and writing out a list of goals. It can become the blueprint for an exciting and rewarding life."

It is amazing what a person can accomplish when he or she sets realistic goals. But as my friend Zig Ziglar says, "It is an admirable attitude to set for yourself the goal of painting the counterpart to the Mona Lisa, but if you flunk Art 101, it is not a reasonable goal."

2. GOALS MUST BE WRITTEN DOWN

In order to accomplish anything you must have a definite goal. Unless you can write it down it isn't definite. It may be a direction, but it isn't a goal.
FRED SMITH

As far as I'm concerned, if your goals aren't written down, they don't really exist. Committing your goals to paper makes them real. That also makes it possible for you to keep track of the progress you're making and enables you to modify your objectives as the need arises.

After you've written your goals on paper, don't stick that paper in a drawer and forget about it. Keep it close at hand, where you can get it out and read it from time to time. I suggest that you review your goals at least once a week to remind yourself what you want to accomplish, check on the progress you're making, and revise them as your situation changes.

I also believe that each of your goals should be no more than one sentence long. If you can't state your goal in one sentence, then you're not stating it properly.

Some people never achieve their goals because they don't really know what their goals are. They have some nebulous ideas about what they want to do, but they've never taken the time to crystallize them into clear, succinct ideas. I have specific goals in a number of areas. For example, there are one hundred books I want to write on topics such as leadership, self-improvement, teamwork, and success. I also have two hundred books arranged by topic, sitting on my office bookshelf, that I want to read before the year is out. I am very precise in what I want to do.

Let's say a young woman named Kathy has an idea that she'd like to learn how to play the guitar. She thinks that she might take lessons someday . . . maybe . . . but she's not sure when. In that case, learning to play the guitar is not really one of Kathy's goals. It would be a goal if she wrote it down this way: "I will learn how to play the guitar by taking lessons, beginning on the first of next month." Only when Kathy's goal is clear and specific can she begin taking steps toward its accomplishment.

WHATEVER YOUR GOALS MAY BE, WRITING THEM DOWN HELPS TO FOCUS YOUR ATTENTION.

Not long ago, I had the privilege of emceeing a dinner where R. C. Sproul, the well-known author and theologian, was the featured speaker. Now, everyone thinks of R. C. Sproul as a highly intelligent and thoughtful person, and he is. But I have discovered that he is also a very colorful and friendly man. He told me that every year, he sets a new, major goal for himself. One year, he learned how to ballroom dance. Another year, he learned to play the violin. He is determined to keep on growing and learning every year, to experience as much of life as he possibly can. What a terrific example!

Whatever your goals may be, writing them down helps to focus your attention. It is like flipping a switch that allows an electrical current to flow, giving you the power needed to move forward. Writing down your goals can be the first step toward achieving them, serving as a tangible reminder of what you want to accomplish. Unless goals are written down, they are often forgotten.

I have spent many years asking the questions, "What does it take to become a success in life?" "What made the difference for you? When did you turn the corner toward success?"

Often, the answer has been, "My life changed the day I first wrote down my goals." I have even heard it said, "The difference between a wish and a goal is that a goal is written down."

Despite what you might hear from fairy tales and Walt Disney movies, wishes rarely come true. On the other hand, properly constructed goals can change your life.

3. Goals Must Be Specific Enough to Measure

*In the absence of clearly defined goals, we become
strangely loyal to performing daily acts of trivia.*
Ernie Banks

The following is not a measurable goal: "I want to learn how to play a musical instrument." This raises too many unanswered questions. What instrument do you want to play? What do you plan to do to learn how to play it? When will you do it?

Here is the same goal, rewritten in a measurable way: "I will learn how to play the tuba by enrolling in Dave's Tuba School this September." If October rolls around, and you haven't taken your first tuba lesson, you know you're not on the way to achieving your goal.

Or suppose you want to lose weight. It's not enough to say, "My goal is to lose some weight." Rather, it would be, "My goal is to lose twenty pounds by March 15." The first statement is not specific or measurable. It allows plenty of wiggle room: "Well, I didn't lose any weight this week, but I'll try to do better next week." For a goal to be effective, it must put pressure on you to act by a certain date.

Suppose you wanted to take a trip across the United States, from California to New York. You wouldn't just get in your car and start driving east, figuring that you'd reach your destination sooner or later.

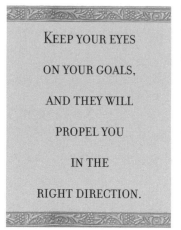

KEEP YOUR EYES ON YOUR GOALS, AND THEY WILL PROPEL YOU IN THE RIGHT DIRECTION.

Instead, you'd get out a map of the United States to see which roads you needed to take. You'd probably decide how far you wanted to drive each day, figure out how long it was going to take you to make the trip, and even make motel reservations in communities along the way. That is what it means to set clear, specific, achievable goals.

Our twenty-year-old daughter, Caroline, was married in October 2003, to a young man named Dimitry, a chaplain in the United States Navy. Dimitry is stationed at Camp

Pendleton, California, which is a long way from Orlando, Florida, where their wedding was celebrated. Ruth and I were understandably concerned about our daughter and son-in-law making that long trip across the country all by themselves. To make sure they knew exactly where they were going, we bought a map of the United States, and Ruth traced their route with a yellow marker. They drove out of Orlando one night about ten, with instructions to call us when they reached the city of Ocala, which is about an hour north of Orlando.

It was after midnight when the phone rang, and Caroline said, "Mommy, Daddy . . . we're in Vero Beach." Vero Beach? I tried to be calm as I explained that they had been going south—in the opposite direction of where they needed to go! They had gone more than three hours out of their way!

This is what happens to us when we don't set goals for ourselves or when we don't do what's necessary to achieve those goals. We wind up far from the path we need to travel. Thankfully, Caroline and Dimitry turned around and didn't have any further trouble the rest of the way to California. From Vero Beach on, they paid attention to the map we'd given them.

Keep your eyes on your goals, and they will propel you in the right direction.

In any organization, you'll find people who leave right at quitting time every day, and you'll find others who never seem to leave before eight, nine, or even later. That's not *always* due to an unequal distribution of the workload or because those who spend more hours in the office are working harder.

Sometimes, it's a matter of setting goals and sticking with them. The person who works a forty-hour week may accomplish more than the guy who works twice that long, simply because he refuses to allow himself to be distracted from the goals at hand. He stays focused on what is really important.

Now, I'm not saying that every person who works long hours does so because he or she hasn't set proper goals. My point is that having proper goals, and staying focused on them, can enable you to accomplish more in a shorter time. That's because it helps you stay focused on things that are really important.

One reason some people don't get what they want out of life is that they aren't really sure what they want. Instead, they settle for whatever comes along. I challenge you today not to settle. Decide what you want to do—for God, for your country, for your family, and for yourself—and then resolve that you won't give up until you do it.

4. Goals Must Have a Deadline
I don't need time. What I need is a deadline.
Duke Ellington

I love this quote from Zig Ziglar: "A goal is a dream with a deadline attached."

How true!

Suppose you want to design your own Web page, but you don't have any idea how to go about it. You decide that you'd like to enroll in a class on Web design at the community college, so you write that down as a goal—but without a deadline attached. How likely is it that you'll actually enroll in that class?

Not very.

Without a deadline, I can almost guarantee you that something more urgent or important will come along to keep you from going to the college and signing up for that class. You may have that same goal for five or ten years, yet never get a step closer to achieving it.

But if you decide to enroll in the class for the fall semester—or if you commit yourself to having a Web site by the first of the year—you'll be forced to act. You won't be able to fool yourself into thinking you're making progress when you're really standing still.

I think of a friend who got married during her senior year of college. She planned to go back to school and get her degree within a couple of years. Now, fifteen years later, she's nearly forty years old, has three teenage children, and is still talking about going back and getting that degree. Unless she attaches a deadline to that goal, I doubt that it will ever happen.

I also have an acquaintance who is a newspaper reporter. For at least twenty years, his goal has been to take some time off and write a screenplay. He's never done it because there's always a breaking news story to cover. Besides, he works long hours on the job, he's involved in a variety of committees at church, and there's always some work around the house that needs his attention. He is in his midfifties now, and I doubt very much if he'll ever achieve his dream of writing a screenplay.

Now, it could be that he doesn't have it within him to write a box-office hit. But it also could be that he'd write a classic that would give renewed hope to millions of people. The sad thing is that he'll probably never know, because he'll probably never get around to trying.

I'm not saying that getting married and raising children isn't important. It is. Nor am I saying that being a newspaper reporter is less significant than being a successful screenwriter. My point is that life is hectic—especially now, when it seems that we are all working harder than ever before, and most of us have very little time left for leisure activities. It is possible to drown in the busyness of day-to-day activities and never get around to doing what you really want to do.

Who can tell what you might be able to accomplish if you write out a goal, set a deadline, and then get to work to meet that deadline? You may not be the greatest screenwriter (or anything else) the world has ever seen. But then again, you might be!

5. Goals Must Be Broken into Short-Term and Long-Term Goals

Mountain climbers don't start climbing from the bottom of the mountain. They look at where they want to go and work backward to where they're starting from.
WARREN BENNIS

What do you want to accomplish within the next month? The next year? The next five years? Where do you want to be twenty-five years from now?

Have you thought about it?

Most people haven't. And that's too bad. Because even though twenty-five years may seem very far into the future, time passes quicker than you may realize. The future is coming whether you're ready or not, so you might as well get ready.

I mentioned earlier that setting goals is a lot like following a road map. If you're planning a trip across the country, the first thing you have to know is which way to turn when you pull out of your driveway. That's only the beginning of the trip—but it's an important part of attaining your long-term goal, which is to reach your destination on the other side of the country.

Again, your short-term goal is to back your car out of the driveway and get it headed in the right direction. Your long-term goal is to make it safely all the way across the country and then back home again.

As the proverb says, "A journey of a thousand miles begins with a single step." That's true in a road trip, and it's also true in a human lifetime. Even Barry Bonds started out in T-ball. I'd go so far as to say that you cannot achieve success in life without having a series of short-range goals to guide you on your way. But neither will you achieve success if you have *only* short-term goals and no overall plan of where you eventually want to be.

First, decide where you want to go. Then figure out how to get there, step by step.

My wife, Ruth, works for Franklin-Covey, so I am well acquainted with Stephen Covey's *7 Habits of Highly Effective*

People. Even though I am still striving to incorporate all seven of those habits into my life, I think I've nailed it on the second one, which states, "Begin with the end in mind." In other words, as you begin drawing up a blueprint, you should already have a vision of the finished building in your mind. As you are planning to start a new church, you picture the doors open and the pews full of worshipers. As you work to bring a professional sports franchise to a city, you picture that team playing before a packed arena.

Sometimes, people don't try to see further ahead than a few weeks or several months at the most. As Penn State football coach Joe Paterno says, "Setting short-range goals may help you win a football game or two. Long-range goals can help you win championships." This is why I suggest that you divide your goals into two categories: short-term goals and long-term goals.

Short-term goals are things you want to achieve today, tomorrow, and this week, on up to the next year, such as completing an art class, taking piano lessons, or reading through the New Testament. Personally, I find that it's helpful to take some time every morning to write down my goals for the day. I write them down in my planner, prioritize them by number, and check them off as I get them done. My list of short-term goals every day includes:

- Reading five newspapers
- Spending an hour doing aerobic exercises

- Taking some time to lift weights

- Spending a certain amount of time doing research for the book I'm working on

- Answering mail and other messages

Throughout the day, I occasionally check that list of goals to see the progress I'm making. Experience has taught me that every hour I spend prioritizing my goals and planning for the day eventually saves me at least three or four hours.

Long-term goals are goals that will take you at least five years into the future, and even further. What do you want to be doing five years from now? Where do you want to be living? Do you want to have a position of leadership in your profession, church, or community? Most of the time,

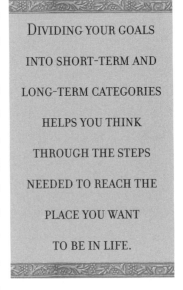

DIVIDING YOUR GOALS INTO SHORT-TERM AND LONG-TERM CATEGORIES HELPS YOU THINK THROUGH THE STEPS NEEDED TO REACH THE PLACE YOU WANT TO BE IN LIFE.

these long-term goals are reached through achieving short-term goals. At the same time, having long-term goals can keep you from becoming discouraged by short-range failures. Defeat in a single battle does not mean the entire war has been lost.

One of my long-term goals is to live to be one hundred years old. I've been working on that one for years—hence the time I spend staying in shape. You can't wait until you're eighty or ninety years old and then decide you want to live to be one hundred. If you want to make it to the century mark, you should probably start working on that goal when you're a teenager.

One of the most important reasons for setting goals is that a goal helps you focus your attention on what you want to achieve. A goal brings things into sharper focus, giving you a clearer picture of what you really want to accomplish. Dividing your goals into short-term and long-term categories helps you think through the steps needed to reach the place you want to be in life.

As we have seen in this building block, setting and striving for goals is an extremely important part of a champion's life. As educator Dr. Benjamin Isaiah Mays says, "The tragedy of life does not lie in not reaching your goals. The tragedy lies in not having any goals to reach."

TAKE RESPONSIBILITY
FOR YOUR ACTIONS

*We are responsible for our own effectiveness, for our own
happiness, and ultimately, for most of our circumstances.*
DR. STEPHEN COVEY

Sometimes it seems that we are living in a world full of victims.
Everyone has a problem—and somebody to blame for their
problem.

But true champions understand that *they* are responsible. For
example, if you experiment with booze and become an alcoholic,
you have no one to blame but yourself. If you smoke cigarettes
and develop lung cancer—once again, that is cause and effect in
action. Nobody is responsible for what you do but you.

I'm reminded of the story of two brothers whose lives took
completely different paths. One became a successful business-
man; the other, a homeless alcoholic. A newspaper reporter
asked the homeless brother why his life had turned out as it had.
"Because my father was a no-good drunk," he answered.

Then he went to the successful brother and asked the same

question. "Because," the fellow said, "my father was a no-good drunk."

One of those brothers had let the circumstances of his life hold him back. The other had used those same circumstances as the fuel to propel him toward success.

Your success depends not so much on what happens to you in life as on what you do with what happens to you in life!

Now, admittedly, there are many things you can't control. You can't control the weather. You can't control the government. Sometimes, you can't control much of anything except your attitude—but that will usually be enough.

Who is responsible for what you say?

You are!

Who is responsible for what you do?

You are!

Who is responsible for what is happening in your life right now?

You are!

Who is responsible for what you do with your life?

You know the answer: you are!

It's true that some people start out with a disadvantage in life. Some are born into poverty. Others are born to parents who are addicted to drugs or alcohol. Still others come into the world with physical and mental disabilities.

It's also true that some people have more than their share of bad luck. But champions don't let misfortune hold them back in life. Instead of whining and complaining about their diffi-culties, they strive to do the best they can with the hand they've been dealt. After all, everyone has setbacks. But life is about 10 percent what happens to you and 90 percent what you do with what happens to you.

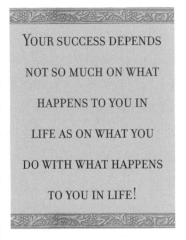

YOUR SUCCESS DEPENDS NOT SO MUCH ON WHAT HAPPENS TO YOU IN LIFE AS ON WHAT YOU DO WITH WHAT HAPPENS TO YOU IN LIFE!

When I was a young man, the experts said that most criminals were a product of their environ-ment. People turned to crime be-cause they grew up in poor neighborhoods. They were violent because they didn't get the love they needed from their parents. The formula was simple: im-prove the environment, and crime will disappear. We needed schools, jobs, and opportunities for inner-city kids to get in-volved in athletics and other wholesome after-school activities.

During the past forty years, enormous sums of money have been poured into improving those high-crime areas. But you know what? Back in the '60s, nobody had ever heard of a drive-by shooting. We didn't open the newspaper in the morning to find an article about fifteen-year-old boys being shot because they didn't come from the right neighborhood. In many areas, people didn't even think about locking their doors if they were only going out for an hour or so.

Have things improved?

No way!

In my opinion, things haven't gotten better because we have forgotten one important thing: in the end, we are all responsible for our own actions. In the words of author Aldous Huxley, "There's only one corner of the universe you can be certain of improving, and that's your own self." Please don't get me wrong. I'm totally in favor of working to improve poor neighborhoods. I think it's very important to build schools, provide jobs, and offer beneficial after-school activities to children. But none of those things will make much of a difference unless we start teaching personal responsibility. In the end, you and you alone are responsible for what happens in your life.

What are you responsible for?

1. YOU ARE RESPONSIBLE FOR YOUR ACTIONS.

2. YOU ARE RESPONSIBLE FOR YOUR DECISIONS.

3. YOU ARE RESPONSIBLE FOR YOUR OWN HAPPINESS.

4. YOU ARE RESPONSIBLE FOR THE WELFARE OF THE WEAK.

5. YOU ARE RESPONSIBLE FOR YOUR RELATIONSHIP WITH GOD.

1. You Are Responsible for Your Actions

In the final analysis, the one quality that all successful people have . . . is the ability to take on responsibility.
Michael Korda

Did you read about the jury that awarded a cigarette smoker nearly one billion dollars in damages because he developed lung cancer?

Personally, I thought it was ridiculous.

Of course, I feel sorry for the gentleman who contracted cancer. And I'm not a big fan of the tobacco industry. But unless I'm missing the point, nobody forced that man to smoke cigarettes. In fact, for many years now, every pack of cigarettes has carried a warning from the U.S. Surgeon General clearly stating that smoking can cause cancer.

Whatever happened to personal responsibility?

Because I believe that we are, for the most part, responsible for what happens to us, I was pleased to read recently that a judge had dismissed a class-action suit against McDonald's and other fast-food restaurants. Attorneys who filed the suit accused the fast-food companies of making people fat and unhealthy.

Excuse me? Didn't those overweight folks know what was going to happen to them if they had a steady diet of cheeseburgers, french fries, and milkshakes?

Brian Cashman, who grew up to become general manager of the New York Yankees, remembers a time in high school when he got into trouble with a BB gun. A friend was shooting at the tires of cars passing by and said to Cashman, "Give it a try." But Cashman's shot was way off the mark. Instead of hitting the tire, it blew out a car's side window.

Cashman remembers that incident as a pivotal moment in his life. "Do I run?" he asked himself. Instead, he went to the car's driver and confessed what he had done. He recalls, "I took total responsibility. Together, we went to the principal, and I asked for forgiveness. That probably saved me from getting expelled. Who knows what direction my life would have taken if that had happened?"

When Harry Truman was president, he had a plaque on his desk that read, "The Buck Stops Here." Whatever problems existed during Truman's administration, he accepted full responsibility for them. He didn't try to blame someone else. He was the leader, and that made him responsible. Harry Truman notwithstanding, we human beings have been passing the buck for a very, very long time. In fact, we've been playing "the blame game" since before we were booted out of the Garden of Eden.

When God asked Adam why he had taken a big bite of the forbidden fruit, Adam pointed his finger at his wife, Eve. When God asked Eve for an explanation, she said, "The devil made me do it" (or something like that). Of course, God didn't buy the alibis.

It's no use trying to make excuses to God. He always knows what's really going on. And here's what He has to say about personal responsibility: "Every living soul belongs to me, the father as well as the son—both alike belong to me. The soul who sins is the one who will die" (Ezekiel 18:4). Later in the same chapter, God says: "The righteousness of the righteous man will be credited to him, and the wickedness of the wicked will be charged against him" (verse 20). And, "I will judge you, each one according to his ways" (verse 30).

You see, in ancient Israel, some people thought they could get away with anything, simply because they were born into God's chosen race or because their parents held places of honor in Jewish society. Others believed they didn't have a chance in life because their fathers were not honorable men. They felt they would be punished for the sins of their parents.

Come to think of it, that's how it is today in America, isn't it? Some people have a pious attitude: "I don't have to worry about anything. I grew up in a Christian family. I've always gone to church. I'm sure God's pretty much okay with anything I do." Others believe they are destined to follow their parents into alcoholism, drug addiction, or crime because, after all, the acorn never falls far from the tree. However, none of this is true. As the apostle Paul writes, "So then, each of us will give an account of himself to God" (Romans 14:12).

A few years ago, after I spoke at a convention in Washington, D.C., a woman came up and told me about the time her five-year-old daughter knocked over a glass of milk at breakfast. Mom cleaned up the mess and told her daughter to be careful not to do it again.

"I didn't do it, Mommy."

"Honey, I saw you do it."

"No I didn't!" the little girl protested. "My hand did it!"

Some of us are like that child. We always look for someone or something else to blame, even if it's our own hand.

2. YOU ARE RESPONSIBLE FOR YOUR DECISIONS

The strongest principle of growth lies in human choice.
GEORGE ELIOT

"If all of your friends jumped off the Empire State Building, would you jump too?" Have you ever heard that one? It's been a favorite of American mothers ever since construction of the Empire State Building was completed in the 1930s.

I have no idea what mothers said before then. Maybe something like, "If all your friends jumped into the Grand Canyon, would you do it too?" (Probably, in ancient Egypt, moms were telling their kids, "If all your friends jumped off the Great Pyramid . . .")

I'm not going to presume that people would jump off tall buildings just because their friends were doing it. At the same time, it occurs to me that most of the problems people go through are caused by wrong decisions.

- A man makes a decision to drink and drive, and someone else is injured or dies as a result.

- A woman decides to start smoking and later suffers from emphysema or lung cancer.

- A young couple decides to buy things they don't really need and then finds themselves hopelessly in debt and harassed by bill collectors.

- A college student spends more time partying than studying and ends up on academic probation, or even expelled from school.

I could give you hundreds of ways I've seen people mess up their lives by making similar decisions. Sometimes, the bad choices aren't so obvious or so big. Several little wrong decisions can combine to take us down the wrong path and eventually get us into deep trouble.

I think of one acquaintance who had an incredible run of "bad luck." He was the sort of guy who seemed to have a black cloud hovering over his head all the time. So often I heard him whine, "Why do all these things happen to me?"

Part of the reason was that he was careless. He didn't pay careful attention to the decisions he made. Although he wasn't aware of it, he constantly sabotaged himself through wrong choices. He was constantly putting himself in a position to have bad things happen to him.

I wouldn't go so far as to say that all of our problems result from wrong decisions. It is true that bad things sometimes simply happen to good people. Disease strikes; a house burns down; a job is lost; an automobile crash leaves someone seriously injured. Such things happen to innocent people every day.

But by making the right decisions, we can put ourselves in a better place to have good things happen to us. The late Norman Vincent Peale said, "The greatest power we have is the power of choice. If you've been moping in unhappiness, you can choose to be joyous instead, and lift yourself into joy, by effort. If you tend to be fearful, you can overcome that misery by choosing to have courage. Even in darkest grief, you have a choice. The whole trend and quality of anyone's life is determined, in the long run, by the choices that are made."

Here's something else a champion needs to know. It doesn't matter who you are or what "disadvantages" may be facing you.

BY MAKING THE RIGHT DECISIONS, WE CAN PUT OURSELVES IN A BETTER PLACE TO HAVE GOOD THINGS HAPPEN TO US.

If you make the right decisions, you can do something terrific with your life. Author Peter Koestenbaum says, "Some people are more talented than others. Some are more educationally privileged than others, but we all have the capacity to be great. Greatness comes with recognizing that your potential is limited only by how you choose, how you use your freedom, how resolute you are—in short, by your attitude, and we are all free to choose our attitude."

Has racism held black people back in this country? Absolutely. Yet Dick Parsons rose through the ranks to become

CEO of Time-Warner. He says, "To have a perception that I'm black almost invariably creates barriers in your own mind. I think a lot of black people do that. . . . It never occurred to me that I couldn't do anything." It is important not to see yourself as different from other people—whether that difference is the color of your skin, your height, your weight, your background, your general appearance, or any other thing.

Always tell yourself that no one is better than you for any reason, and you *can* achieve success!

3. YOU ARE RESPONSIBLE FOR YOUR OWN HAPPINESS

*The first thing everyone can do to achieve happiness
is to come to the realization that they have the sole
responsibility for their happiness.*
ZIG ZIGLAR

Champions realize that most of the time, happiness is a choice. (In certain situations, a person may be unhappy because of depression or a chemical imbalance that can be improved by therapy or medication.)

You can't depend on your parents to make you happy.

It's not fair to expect your boyfriend or girlfriend or spouse to make you happy.

You'll wind up disappointed and empty if you depend on things—like cars and clothes—to make you happy.

You'll never get what you need if you require affirmation from others to give you a happy outlook.

And you will not find lasting happiness if the slightest setback can knock the props out from under you, leaving you deflated and depressed.

Make up your mind that you will have a joyful spirit. Strive to see the good side of things. Decide right now that you will not let other people affect the way you view life.

I believe that the happiest people are those who understand that their lives have meaning—that God created them for a special purpose. The late, brilliant psychiatrist Viktor Frankl talked about this in his landmark book, *Man's Search for Meaning*.

Dr. Frankl endured unbelievable atrocities in Nazi concentration camps during World War II. For years, he was surrounded by constant brutality. He and his fellow prisoners knew they could die at any time. They were poorly fed, deprived of sleep, and forced to spend long days in hard labor.

It wasn't surprising, given those circumstances, that some men quickly lost all hope. Many of them simply gave up and died. What was surprising was that others were able to maintain a somewhat positive outlook despite the tortures they endured every day. These were the ones who felt that their lives had meaning, despite the miserable circumstances in which they found themselves. They kept going for the sake of their loved ones. They never gave up hope of being reunited with their friends and families someday. They thought about the careers they had left behind and looked forward to resuming them when the war was over. Their bodies were captive, but their spirits were free to soar.

Frankl wrote, "We who lived in concentration camps can remember the men who walked through the huts, comforting others, giving away their last piece of bread. They may have been few in number, but they offer sufficient proof that everything can be taken from a man but one thing: the last of the human freedoms—to choose one's attitude in any given set of circumstances—to choose one's own way."

You see, there are many, many situations in life that are beyond our ability to control. I long ago came to the realization that I can't do much of anything about the weather. I can't single-handedly fix the hole in the ozone layer. I can't fix the economic woes of every country in South America. I can't prevent earthquakes, floods, or hurricanes.

That's why, about five years ago, I called a press conference and announced that I was resigning as "general manager of the universe." Of course, it was big news when I let everyone know that from now on, I was going to let God handle all those things as He saw fit, and I was only going to be responsible for one thing: my attitude.

Ever since then, my life has been a whole lot better. If you're still feeling responsible for everyone and everything, perhaps it's time *you* call a press conference and resign as general manager of the universe. Believe me, you won't regret it.

4. YOU ARE RESPONSIBLE FOR THE WELFARE OF THE WEAK

*I never look at feeding the masses as my responsibility. I look
at the individual. I can love only one person at a time. I can
feed only one person at a time. Just one, one, one. . . .
Same thing for you. Just begin—one, one, one.*
MOTHER TERESA

Jesus was clear on the matter: God expects us to do what we can
to help the poor—those who are hungry, ragged, sick, or suffering in any other way. Referring to those who help the weak
and suffering, Jesus said, "Whatever you did for one of the least
of these brothers of mine, you did for me" (Matthew 25:40).

In saying this, Jesus was reaffirming dozens of teachings
found throughout the Old Testament. One of my favorites is
found in the fifty-eighth chapter of Isaiah:

> Is not this the kind of fasting I have chosen: to loose the
> chains of injustice and untie the cords of the yoke, to set the
> oppressed free and break every yoke? Is it not to share your
> food with the hungry and to provide the poor wanderer with
> shelter—when you see the naked, to clothe him, and not to
> turn away from your own flesh and blood? Then your light
> will break forth like the dawn, and your healing will quickly
> appear; then your righteousness will go before you, and the
> glory of the LORD will be your rear guard. (verses 6–8)

Again, it is clear that God expects us, as His people, to do
what we can to assist the poor and needy. It is true, that as

Jesus said, there will always be people who are poor (see Matthew 26:11). But that statement does not excuse us from doing whatever we can to help them.

I'm not suggesting that you should devote your life totally to helping the poor. If God has called you to do that, by all means, do it. But whatever your calling may be, if you want to live in a way that is pleasing to God, then helping the poor must be a regular part of what you do.

Remember: helping the poor is not the government's job.

It's not the church's job.

It's not the United Way's job.

It's my job—and it's your job!

I know that sometimes, when we look around at the poverty that exists in the world, it appears to be hopeless. It seems that no matter what you do, you can't make a real difference. Yet, while we don't have the means to help all the poor people, we do have the means to help some of them.

There are many ways you can show responsibility for the poor and weak. You can:

- Donate time or give money to the local rescue mission or homeless shelter.

- Sponsor a child through World Vision, Compassion International, or a similar organization.

- Be a Big Brother or Big Sister to a child who needs a guiding hand.

- Volunteer some time to an adult literacy program.

- Become a regular visitor at the nearest nursing home.

I'm sure you can think of many other ways you can reach out to those who need to know that someone cares about them. You can't do it all. But you can do something—and that will be enough.

Just before Christmas last year, a man named C. R. Smith died in Orlando at the age of seventy-seven. Smith, who was often referred to as "The Mother Teresa of Orlando," will forever be remembered as the founder of Frontline Ministries.

Back in the mid-1960s, Smith owned three successful appliance stores in the Orlando area. But he knew that God was calling him to do something more than sell refrigerators and washing machines. In a time of racial unrest, Smith was a white man who felt called to extend a helping hand to poor black kids growing up in Orlando's inner city. Frontline started out as a part-time ministry. All Smith had was a pickup truck, from which he handed out tuna sandwiches and Kool-Aid. Eventually, Frontline became Smith's life's work.

During the next thirty years, thousands of young people were positively affected by Smith's efforts. In fact, just about every person who grew up in West Orlando between 1967 and 2003 was touched in some way by his work.

C. R. Smith was a kind, generous man who gave his life to helping others—a man who never allowed himself to think,

What can one man do? He proved that one person can do an awful lot.

5. YOU ARE RESPONSIBLE FOR YOUR RELATIONSHIP WITH GOD

Whoever is on God's side is on the winning side, and cannot lose. Whoever is on the other side is on the losing side, and cannot win. Here there is no chance; no gamble. There is freedom to choose whose side we shall be on, but no freedom to negotiate the results of that choice, once it is made.
A. W. TOZER

Did you grow up in a Christian home? Did your parents make sure you were in church every time the doors were open?

Good for them. But your past church attendance doesn't matter all that much to God. He is not content to have a connection with you that exists only because of your parents' beliefs.

You see, God doesn't have any grandchildren. He's not content to be a "distant relative" you barely know. He wants to have a personal, intimate relationship with you. If you don't have that kind of relationship with God, please go back to the introduction and reread what I said about the importance of surrendering your life to Christ.

The Bible says, in Romans 10:9, "If you confess with your mouth, 'Jesus is Lord,' and believe in your heart that God raised him from the dead, you will be saved."

Do you believe that Jesus Christ died on your behalf? If so, all you need to do is tell Him so and ask Him to be your Savior and Lord. This is such an important decision. Please don't put it off.

Once you have surrendered your life to Christ, you can say with the apostle John: "How great is the love the Father has lavished on us, that we should be called children of God! And that is what we are!" (1 John 3:1).

CHOOSE THE RIGHT KINDS OF FRIENDS

Cultivate wrong friendships and you're a goner.
That is why we're warned not to be deceived
regarding the danger of wrong associations.
Without realizing it, we could be playing with fire.
CHARLES SWINDOLL

To a great degree, the kinds of friends you choose will determine the course of your life. If you choose to surround yourself with positive, upbeat people, they will lift you up. But if you choose to hang out with people who are negative, dishonest, and immoral, then you will most likely be dragged into the gutter along with them.

As the Bible says, "Bad company corrupts good character" (1 Corinthians 15:33). It never fails. You can't choose your relatives, but you *can* choose your friends. Because that is the case, choose wisely.

In a moment, we're going to talk about how to be successful when it comes to choosing your friends. But first, I want to touch on something else that is vitally important. In order to *have* a friend, you first have to *be* a friend. In other words, you can't get friendship from someone else if you're not willing to give your friendship in return.

Throughout His earthly ministry, Jesus fulfilled the role of being a true friend to His disciples. He loved them unconditionally, no matter what they did. He was patient with them when their stubbornness and thickheadedness would have driven anyone else up the nearest wall—yet He always told them the truth, even when they didn't want to hear it. And then, at the Last Supper, He demonstrated the connection between friendship and servanthood by humbly washing the disciples' feet. In performing this act, Christ was taking on a job that was usually reserved for the lowest-ranking household servant.

Imagine how you'd feel if tomorrow was the day to put your trash cans out on the curb for pickup, and when the truck came through your neighborhood, you discovered that Jesus Himself had taken on the job of a garbage collector. What if, in fact, He was the one whose job it was to ride on the back of the truck, jumping off every thirty feet or so to pick up and dump another garbage can? Would you let Him empty your garbage?

I don't think so. You'd be out in the street, trying to grab your trash can away from Him. "Here, Lord, I'll empty this for You. You've got more important things to do. No, Lord, please. Don't bother with my trash. Just leave it alone."

It's an absurd picture, I know. But it helps me understand how the disciples felt when Jesus got a basin of water, tied a towel around His waist, and began to wash their feet. They were aghast that the Son of God would even think of doing such a thing. But He did it because He loved them—and because He loved us. He wanted to set an example of what true friends are willing to do for one another.

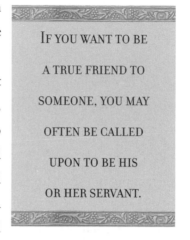

IF YOU WANT TO BE A TRUE FRIEND TO SOMEONE, YOU MAY OFTEN BE CALLED UPON TO BE HIS OR HER SERVANT.

I have found that if you want to be a true friend to someone, you may often be called upon to be his or her servant. A true friend doesn't limit his behavior toward another on the basis of pride. A friend is there whenever you need him, to do whatever he can for you. If you need him to wash your feet, he'll do it. If you need her to sit up with you because you're feeling blue, she'll do that too.

The thirteenth chapter of 1 Corinthians describes the love that ought to be lived out between friends who share the common bond of faith in Christ: "Love is patient, love is kind. It does not envy, it does not boast, it is not proud. It is not rude, it is not self-seeking, it is not easily angered, it keeps no record of wrongs. Love does not delight in evil but rejoices with the truth. It always protects, always trusts, always hopes, always perseveres. Love never fails" (verses 4–8).

Wow! That's a pretty high mark to aim for, isn't it? Yet that is the kind of love God has for us, and, with His help, it is the kind of love we can show to others.

Perhaps you have heard of Dwight L. Moody. He was the Billy Graham of the late 1800s, and Moody Bible Institute, in Chicago, bears his name.

One year, when Dr. Moody was at the height of his fame, a group of preachers from Europe attended his Northfield Bible Conference in Massachusetts. The first night of the conference, as the world-famous preacher was walking the halls of the dormitory, he saw that many of the European visitors had placed their shoes in the hall outside their rooms. Dr. Moody realized that they were expecting the "hall servants" to take their shoes and polish them, as was the custom in Europe. However, there were no hall servants in America.

Dr. Moody did not want his guests to be disappointed. He tried to get some Bible students to help polish the shoes, but everyone he asked had an excuse about why he couldn't help. Nobody said so in so many words, but the attitude seemed to be that the task was beneath them. Shining other people's shoes just wasn't something a dignified person would do.

So he gathered up the shoes, took them back to his room, and began to polish and shine them himself. No one would have known about it, except that a friend of Dr. Moody's dropped by and caught him in the act.

The two of them finished the job and carefully placed the

shoes back outside the appropriate doors. The visitors from Europe never found out who had shined their shoes. Dr. Moody didn't want anyone to know what he had done. His friend, however, did tell a few people—and for the rest of the conference, the shoes were taken in and polished every night—by men whose hearts had been touched by the great evangelist's humility and spirit of true friendship toward others.

Wouldn't it be great to have a friend like that? And wouldn't it be great to *be* a friend like that?

What qualities should we look for in our friends?

1. CHOOSE FRIENDS WHO WILL BRING OUT THE BEST IN YOU.

2. CHOOSE FRIENDS WHO ARE BELIEVERS.

3. CHOOSE FRIENDS WHO ARE WISE.

4. CHOOSE FRIENDS WHO WILL BE LOYAL TO YOU NO MATTER WHAT.

5. CHOOSE FRIENDS WHO MAKE YOU FEEL BETTER ABOUT YOURSELF.

Let's look at these five characteristics as we answer the question, "How can you choose the right kinds of friends?"

1. CHOOSE FRIENDS WHO WILL BRING OUT THE BEST IN YOU

Your best friend is he who brings out
the best that is within you.
HENRY FORD

Motivational speaker Charlie "Tremendous" Jones was right on target when he said, "If you hang around achievers, you will be a better achiever; hang around thinkers and you will be a better thinker; hang around givers and you will be a better giver; but hang around a bunch of thumb-sucking complaining boneheads and you will be a better thumb-sucking complaining bonehead."

Talk about telling it like it is!

Our son Alan was grounded for his entire junior and senior years of high school because he could not get away from the bad influence of another boy in his class. When the two of them got together, something bad was bound to happen—and usually did. When Alan was by himself, or when he was hanging out with other friends, he was fine. But put Alan and this other boy together, and they became a deadly duo—like famine and pestilence.

Almost every time one of our kids has gotten into trouble at school, it has turned out to be a group effort. I have seen again and again and again the effect that friends can have on a person's behavior—for good or bad.

Have you ever heard that a man and woman who have been married to each other for a long time will start to look alike? I think that's probably true. (But please don't tell my beautiful wife,

Ruth.) I'm convinced that over time, we begin to look like our friends. Perhaps not physically—but certainly spiritually.

A study by Purdue University found that nearly two-thirds of America's teenagers would go along with the actions of a crowd, even if they thought what the crowd was doing was wrong. How do you feel about that? Do you have friends you can count on to help you do the right thing at all times?

Not long ago, I read a story in the newspaper about a young man who is facing jail time in Nevada—apparently because he went along with the crowd. He's in trouble because John Robinson, head football coach at the University of Nevada–Las Vegas, was hit on the head by a crumpled-up beer can thrown from the stands during a game in Reno.

Police arrested the young man for throwing the can.

But in the news article, the fellow said he was only doing what everyone else was doing. The other fans were throwing things, so he threw something too. "How do they know it was my can that hit him?" he asked. "How can they possibly charge me with a crime, when I was just doing what everyone else was doing?" In other words, "It's not fair!"

Have you ever had something like that happen to you? You did something because everyone else was doing it, and you were the one who got caught. Ever feel like you can't get away with anything?

Well, in the end, none of us can get away with wrong behavior. (God knows all about it anyway.) So it is important to have friends who encourage us to do well rather than friends who dare us to join them in behavior we know is wrong.

California's giant redwood trees may grow to be two hundred feet tall. They are the tallest trees in the world. Yet they have very shallow root systems. A redwood standing all by itself could easily be blown over by a strong wind. That's why you will almost always see a cluster of redwoods growing together. Their roots intertwine, and the group is able to stand strong as the wind howls around them.

Good friends are the same way. They give us shelter and help us stand strong and tall, even when winds of adversity are blowing against us.

2. CHOOSE FRIENDS WHO ARE BELIEVERS

As the wrong friends can steer us toward evil, godly companions can help us stay on the right path. Good friends will keep us turned toward God.
RANDY RAYSBROOK

The way I see it, one of the very best places to find friends is at church—or at a church-related activity.

Of course, just because someone is at church doesn't mean he or she is a good person. Almost every congregation has a few phonies and people who want to be good but aren't. A church is not a museum for saints but a hospital for sinners.

Having admitted that those who attend church aren't necessarily perfect, I will also say that, percentage-wise, I'm sure you'll find more good people at church than you will at any other place in your community.

If you are a Christian, you ought to have Christian friends. That doesn't mean you shouldn't develop friendships with people who are not believers. After all, being a friend to someone is the very best way to help that person see God's love. But if you are a Christian who has no Christian friends, you are at risk of drifting into dangerous waters. You need to have friends who share your faith, friends you can lean on in times of trouble, friends who can support you and help you remember to keep your eyes on the Lord.

> IT IS IMPORTANT TO HAVE FRIENDS WHO ENCOURAGE US TO DO WELL RATHER THAN FRIENDS WHO DARE US TO JOIN THEM IN BEHAVIOR WE KNOW IS WRONG.

Author and Pastor David Jeremiah says, "Sometimes Christians forge friendships with unwise people, thinking they can change them, but you will both be changed. Many Christian young people marry non-Christians, thinking they can win them over after the marriage. It rarely happens." He goes on to say, "You shouldn't make committed friendships with fools, but you should look for faithful friends."

Len Bias was a terrific basketball player at the University of Maryland. He was a cinch to be a high draft choice in the National Basketball Association's draft of 1986. Bias was also a born-again Christian. Everyone knew that he was a "straight arrow."

But some of his Christian friends were worried about him. Bias's skill with a basketball had brought him national fame, and it had also brought him dozens of new friends, some of whom were undesirable. Those new friends told Len that he ought to live a little. They wanted him to try cocaine, so he did.

And it killed him—two days after the NBA draft. Len Bias died before his twenty-first birthday because cocaine stopped his heart. What a terrible waste of a life. And it never would have happened if he had not surrounded himself with the wrong kind of friends.

I realize that what I'm saying may sound extreme. I wouldn't blame you if you were thinking, *Oh, come on now, Pat. Are you saying that if I choose non-Christian friends, I'm going to wind up dead of a drug overdose?*

Of course not. I realize that what happened to Len Bias is an extreme example. And I've never been one for using scare tactics. Still, the principle applies. As an executive with a Major League sports franchise, I've seen it happen many times. If you hang around with bad people, it's almost certain that eventually they'll drag you down. If you hang out with other believers, you will find your faith growing stronger.

Nowhere in the Bible will you find a command to attend church on Sunday. But it is clear from Scripture that the early Christians met together on a regular basis. Acts 2:46 says, "Every day they continued to meet together in the temple courts." The author of Hebrews wrote, "Let us not give up meeting together, as some are in the habit of doing, but let us encourage one another—and all the more as you see the Day approaching" (Hebrews 10:25).

It was important for Christians in the first century to get together on a regular basis, and it's just as important for Christians of the twenty-first century. Why? First, it's important for believers to worship God together. Secondly, it is crucial for believers to encourage, support, and draw strength from one another.

3. CHOOSE FRIENDS WHO ARE WISE

He who walks with the wise grows wise,
but a companion of fools suffers harm.
PROVERBS 13:20

The world we live in—the world God created for us—is overflowing with wonderful and beautiful things, just waiting to be discovered. Tragically, some people go through life with blinders on. They never learn how to see further than their daily routine. They get up in the morning and go to work. They come home in the evening and watch television until bedtime. Then they get up the next morning and do it all over again. They never even notice the wonders that exist all around them.

They've never stood transfixed in front of a painting by Van Gogh or da Vinci in an art museum. They have never learned to appreciate God's wonderful gifts of color and artistry.

They've never been moved to tears by a symphony composed by Beethoven or Tchaikovsky. Somehow, they've overlooked the beauty of music, another of God's great gifts.

They've never spent a clear summer evening just sitting out in the backyard, looking up at the stars and marveling at the vastness of our universe.

I'm not an expert about art, music, or astronomy—but I have friends who can help me gain a better understanding of and appreciation in each of these areas. You can learn so much by choosing friends who are wise in areas where you are less knowledgeable.

If you can't hang out with brilliant people, you can learn from them by reading the books they've written. For example, I can't spend time with C. S. Lewis because he is dead. But I can get to know his ideas through the books he wrote. If I called Condoleezza Rice and invited her to come over for dinner, she probably wouldn't be able, or inclined, to come. She's busy serving as secretary of state. But I can read books about her and written by her, and learn as much from her in this way as I could during several dinners together.

Best-selling author Tom Peters understands this. He says that whenever he packs his suitcase for a trip, it takes him only a few minutes to choose the clothes he's going to take along. But, "It takes somewhere between several hours and several days to choose the books. I take along a dozen for a four or five-day trip." Through books we can read the great ideas of the smartest men and women who have ever lived!

4. CHOOSE FRIENDS WHO WILL BE LOYAL TO YOU NO MATTER WHAT

The friend in my adversity I shall always cherish most.
I can better trust those who helped to relieve the gloom
of my dark hours than those who are so ready to enjoy
with me the sunshine of my prosperity.
ULYSSES S. GRANT

How can you tell that someone will be loyal to you no matter what? Unfortunately, you can't. Not at first anyway. But as time goes by, as you experience success and failure in life, those qualities will become apparent.

Friends who don't really care about you will desert you at the first sign of trouble. True-blue friends will stick with you when everyone else has deserted you. They care about you just because they care about you, and not because you can do something for them.

Jesus said, "Greater love has no one than this, that he lay down his life for his friends" (John 15:13). To be honest, I'm not too sure very many people have friends who would be willing to die for them. Even Jesus's supposedly loyal disciples took off like a bunch of scared rabbits when He was arrested. But it's not too much to expect that your friends will be willing to make occasional sacrifices for you. For example:

- A true friend doesn't always have to have the last word in an argument. He is willing to let you win once in a while.

- A true friend doesn't expect you to pay for everything all the time. Even if you insist on paying, he'll grab the check occasionally.

- A true friend won't ask you to do anything that is against your principles or that can get you into trouble.

- A true friend tries hard not to say, "I told you so," even when she *has* told you so.

- A true friend tries his best to keep you out of trouble.

- A true friend is delighted by your successes. She is not jealous or resentful, but she rejoices with you.

- A true friend does not demand that you spend all your time with him. Friendship is not possessive.

- A true friend sticks up for you when you're not around to defend yourself. She doesn't talk about you behind your back or listen to others who speak unkindly about you.

- A true friend is willing to let you be a human being. He knows that humans mess up once in a while, and he forgives you when you do.

In other words, a so-called friend who is always the taker and who expects you to always be the giver is no friend at all. That should be obvious, but it's not. During my years in professional sports, I've seen many men get into trouble because they couldn't tell the difference between friends and hangers-on. They had "friends" who were ready to help them spend their money on booze, drugs, and living large. But when all that wild living got them into trouble with the law or diminished their skills so they were no longer able to command those big, fat contracts, their so-called friends disappeared faster than an ice cube on an Orlando sidewalk in August!

True friends will be loyal to you and continue to love you—no matter what.

5. CHOOSE FRIENDS WHO MAKE YOU FEEL BETTER ABOUT YOURSELF

Our true friends give us comfort in sorrow, strength in adversity, courage in crisis, and fortitude for failure.
WILLIAM ARTHUR WARD

Why would people want to spend time with friends who make them feel bad about themselves? I don't know the answer to that question. But I do know that a lot of people do it.

I think this is especially true of young women who are mistreated by their boyfriends. But whether it's a platonic friendship or a serious romance, nobody needs to be around someone who abuses or belittles them verbally or assaults them physically.

If you are in such a relationship, please, *end it now.*

If you are in an unhealthy relationship, you cannot afford to fool yourself into thinking that things will get better over time. That seldom happens—they will only get worse. The best thing to do about unhealthy relationships is to let them go, no matter how much it may hurt.

I'm not suggesting that your friends should spend all their

time trying to build you up. But neither should they spend all their time trying to tear you down. Once in a while, even the best of friends may be angry, argumentative, or overcritical. A good friend may have a down day and be sad or depressed. But a good friend will not be in an angry, harsh mood all the time.

I won't name names, but I know some married couples who are just horrible to be around because they keep zinging each other all the time. Whenever I am obligated to spend some time with folks like that, I always think, *How did your marriage come to this?* And then I realize that it must have been this way from the start.

What a lousy way to spend your life: married to someone whom you obviously don't like very much and being constantly reminded that your spouse doesn't exactly worship the ground you walk on either!

Before we move on to the next building block for championship living, I want to mention one other important fact about friendship.

Although we are naturally drawn to people who share our interests, it is not necessary—at all—for friends to have a great deal in common. People who are quite different can be the best of friends. They just enjoy being together—and even if they don't find much to talk about, they are comfortable in the silence.

When the brilliant physicist Albert Einstein was on the faculty at Princeton, a little girl used to stop by his office to visit with him for a few minutes almost every afternoon. One day, the girl's mother met Einstein while he was taking a walk and asked if her daughter's visits bothered him.

"Oh no, not at all," he said.

"But what do you talk about?" the mom asked. She wondered how a brilliant scientist and a little girl could possibly find anything in common.

"Sometimes, we don't talk much at all," Einstein replied. "But she brings me cookies, and I help her with her arithmetic homework."

They were two very different people, a brilliant older man and a kindhearted little girl, who simply enjoyed spending time with each other.

When we began our discussion of friendship, I stated that in order to have a friend, you had to be one. I'd like to close this building block by presenting these:

TEN COMMANDMENTS OF FRIENDSHIP

1. Hold your tongue. There's no reason to say everything that crosses your mind.

2. Don't make promises you can't keep.

3. Never miss an opportunity to give an encouraging word.

4. Be genuinely interested in others.

5. Don't burden others by constantly talking about your aches, pains, or troubles. Remember that others have aches, pains, and troubles of their own.

6. Keep an open mind regarding the other person's point of view. Strive to avoid an argumentative tone of voice.

7. Don't become involved in gossip about other people.

8. Think about other people's feelings. For example, when you see an opportunity to zing somebody, pass it up. Friendship should take priority over demonstrating your wit.

9. Pay no attention when other people say bad things about you. Let your character speak for itself.

10. Don't worry about getting credit for what you've done. Do your best, and then be patient. Your reward will surely come.

BUILDING BLOCK

TURN FAILURES INTO STRENGTHS

To try something you can't do, to try and fail; then
try again. That, to me, is success. My generation
will be judged by the splendor of our failures.
WILLIAM FAULKNER

The first few years of my professional sports career, it seemed that everything we did turned out right. If we traded for a so-so player, he suddenly became a superstar. If we let a good player get away, he immediately went into a terrible slump. Our teams won, the fans flocked to see them, and everything was great!

Then, sometime in 1973, the Midas touch suddenly seemed to desert me. I was in Chicago, working as general manager of the Bulls, and it seemed that the whole world was ganging up on me. Everything I touched turned to fool's gold.

I was attending Moody Church at the time and scheduled a lunch with my pastor, Warren Wiersbe. I poured out my heart while he sat and listened patiently with an expression of deep sympathy. When I was finished with my catalogue of troubles, he said something I will never forget: "Well, Pat, don't waste your sufferings."

That may have been one of the best life lessons I've ever learned. When troubles come—as they will—make the most of them. Learn from them. Give them to God and allow Him to use them for your benefit. Don't pray that He will take your troubles away. Pray that He will give you strength and patience to endure!

A few years ago, I wrote my autobiography, *Ahead of the Game*. As I looked back over my life, it became clear to me that my greatest advances came through tough times. I believe that's true in most people's lives.

I recently attended a small, private lunch with best-selling author John Maxwell. In his after-lunch remarks, Maxwell said, "Not too long ago, I was asked to speak to four hundred university and college presidents. I said, 'If I was in your shoes, the first thing I'd do is add to the curriculum a course on Failure 101. All of your students are going to fail at some point in life—so let's teach them how to fail properly. They must learn to fall forward."

Maxwell is right. If you haven't experienced failure yet, just wait. It will come. Failures are an inevitable part of life.

Show me someone who has never failed, and I will show you someone who has never tried to do anything. The important thing is not staying away from failure, but, rather, what you do with failure when it comes.

Champions understand that people learn to become better as a result of their setbacks. In this way, they are like the healing bone that becomes stronger at the point where it was broken.

Most of us have heard about the long list of failures Abraham Lincoln endured before he was finally elected president of the United States. He failed in business. He failed in politics again and again. He couldn't seem to do anything right!

Well, Honest Abe wasn't alone. Let me take just a moment to tell you about some other notable failures:

- George Washington lost the first five battles he fought against British troops during the Revolutionary War.

- Winston Churchill failed in business and was blamed for one of Great Britain's costliest defeats in World War I.

- Harry Truman failed so often in business and politics that he once wrote a letter to his wife, Bess, in which he said, "I can't possibly lose forever."

- Louis Pasteur's grade-point average ranked him fifteenth out of twenty-two students in his college chemistry class.

- Beethoven's composition teacher said he was a dunce who couldn't possibly learn anything.

Need some more examples?

- Early in her career, Lucille Ball was fired by a producer who told her, "You're not meant for show business. Go home."

- After an early performance at the Grand Ole Opry, Elvis Presley was told that he should stick to driving a truck since he obviously had no future as a singer.

- Vincent Van Gogh sold only one painting in his lifetime, and that was to his brother, Theodore.

- Rudyard Kipling was fired from his first job as a newspaper reporter because his editor told him, "You don't know how to use the English language."

- After completing his first novel, Stephen King decided it was terrible and threw it into the trash. His wife fished it out and sent it to a publisher. *Carrie* became the work that launched his long, successful career.

- When Bob Dylan first performed at a high-school talent show, his classmates booed him off the stage.

I could go on to give you the names of hundreds of people who tasted failure but bounced back to make a mark on the world. As strange as it may sound, adversity may be one of the best things that can happen to a person. It gives you a whole new perspective on life and makes you stronger.

> ADVERSITY MAY BE ONE OF THE BEST THINGS THAT CAN HAPPEN TO A PERSON.

Arnold Schwarzenegger, the popular actor who became governor of California, is one of the world's strongest men and a former Mr. Universe. He said, "Strength does not come from winning. Your struggles develop your strengths. When you go through hardships and decide not to surrender, that is strength."

If you want to be a champion, here are some important facts you need to know about failure:

1. NOBODY SUCCEEDS ALL THE TIME.

2. IT IS NO DISGRACE TO FALL, BUT IT IS A DISGRACE TO LIE THERE AFTER YOU FALL.

3. FAILURE ISN'T FINAL.

4. FAILURE CAN BE A BETTER TEACHER THAN SUCCESS.

5. GOD'S STRENGTH IS MADE PERFECT IN OUR WEAKNESS.

1. NOBODY SUCCEEDS ALL THE TIME

Mistakes are a fact of life. It is the response to the error that counts.
NIKKI GIOVANNI

Ask people to name the greatest athletes of all time, and one person is certain to be near the top of everyone's list: Michael Jordan.

No wonder. The Chicago Bulls were the best team in any sport throughout most of the 1990s, and Jordan was the primary reason. Time after time, he came through with the game-winning basket—so often, in fact, that if the game was close, everyone just knew that Jordan was going to pull it out with a swisher from the perimeter as time ran out.

Yet Michael Jordan was not good enough to make his high-school basketball team during his sophomore year. He was discouraged and considered giving up the sport altogether, until a pep talk from his mother convinced him to keep trying.

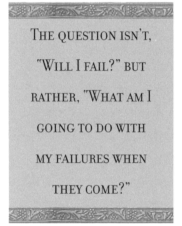

THE QUESTION ISN'T, "WILL I FAIL?" BUT RATHER, "WHAT AM I GOING TO DO WITH MY FAILURES WHEN THEY COME?"

The rest is sports history.

In a television commercial made when Jordan was near the end of his career, he talked about the failures he had experienced. As the camera followed him walking off the court, Jordan said, "I've missed over nine thousand shots in my career. I've lost over three hundred games. Twenty-six times, I've been trusted to take the game-winning shot and missed. I've failed over and over again in my life—and that is why I succeed."

As we've seen, when you fail at something, you're in pretty good company. Yes, you are going to mess things up sometimes. There's no doubt about that. So the question isn't, "Will I fail?" but rather, "What am I going to do with my failures when they come?"

2. It Is No Disgrace to Fall, but It Is a Disgrace to Lie There After You Fall

I don't measure a man's success by how high he climbs
but by how high he bounces when he hits bottom.
George S. Patton

In the early 1960s, a musical group called the Beatles had an audition at Decca Records. The Beatles had gained a sizable following by playing small nightclubs. The boys in the band all knew that getting a recording contract with a company like Decca would be a giant step forward in their career. Also in the studio to audition that day was another band—Brian Poole and the Tremeloes.

Guess which group Decca signed?

That's right: Brian Poole and the boys were snatched up.

As for the Beatles, Decca executive Dick Rowe was not impressed. He didn't think they were all that good. Besides, he said, guitar bands were on the way out.

The Beatles were disappointed, but they picked up their instruments and tried again—at Pye, Columbia, and Philips Records, experiencing rejection at every stop along the way. Finally, they were offered a recording contract by George Martin of Parlophone Records. Martin went on to produce and arrange many of the Beatles' multimillion-selling albums.

John Lennon, Paul McCartney, George Harrison, and Ringo Starr literally changed popular music. But if they had listened to the folks at Decca, the world most likely would have never heard of them.

The Beatles' story brings to mind something Abraham Lincoln said: "My great concern is not whether you failed, but whether you are content with your failures." The Beatles weren't content to fail, and they eventually became one of the greatest musical success stories the world has ever seen.

3. FAILURE ISN'T FINAL

I make more mistakes than anyone else I know,
and sooner or later I patent most of them.
THOMAS ALVA EDISON

Thomas Edison said he tried more than one thousand times, and failed, to invent the electric light. When someone asked him if all those failures made him discouraged, he replied that just the opposite was true. He believed that every failed attempt showed him another way *not* to go and thus led him closer to success.

My boss, Rich De Vos, has been an inspiration to me when it comes to bouncing back from failure. He's been down many times in his life, but he's never been out for the count. Whenever a setback comes along, he takes it in stride and looks for a way to get back on top.

He said, "If I had to select one quality, one personal characteristic that I regard as being the most highly correlated with success—whatever the field, I would pick the trait of persistence . . . determination . . . the will to endure to the end . . . to get knocked down seventy times and get up off the floor saying, 'Here comes number seventy-one.'"

A reporter once asked racing legend Bobby Unser how he handled defeat. He responded, "If you don't learn from losing or doing something wrong, then shame on you. If I lose, I go home and think about why. You can tell a lot about someone by the effort they make when they are down. Some people mope. Winners are proactive. They figure out what they did wrong and don't do it again."

Perhaps you've heard the story about the gentleman who found himself in deep financial distress and began praying that God would help him win the lottery. Every night for a month, he kept praying that he'd win the big prize, but nothing ever happened. One night, as he knelt in prayer, tears began running down his cheeks. "Oh, Lord," he cried, "I've tried so hard to serve you. Why won't you let me win the lottery? I've prayed and prayed but nothing happens. Why aren't you listening?"

Suddenly the house began to shake. A bright light filled the room, and a deep, thundering voice replied: "I have heard your prayer, and I will help you win the lottery. But there is one thing you must do first."

"Anything, Lord. What is it?"

"Buy a ticket!" came the reply.

I know. It's kind of corny. But the principle applies. God can help us overcome any adversity that comes our way, but He expects us to do our part. As someone has said, "Pray like it all depends on God, but work like it all depends on you." That's the best combination I know of for overcoming adversity and bouncing back from failure.

4. FAILURE CAN BE A BETTER TEACHER THAN SUCCESS

To me, success can be achieved only through repeated failure and introspection. In fact, success represents the 1 percent of your work that results from the 99 percent that is called failure.
SOICHIRO HONDA

The late Tennessee Williams achieved great success as a playwright, turning out such successful plays as *A Streetcar Named Desire* and *Cat on a Hot Tin Roof.* When Williams was just starting out as a writer, he sent some short stories to a literary magazine. Within a few weeks, he received a rejection letter with a detailed explanation of why the stories were not suitable for publication.

Naturally, Williams was disappointed. Even so, he immediately sat down and wrote the following letter to the editor who had rejected his work: "Like most young writers, I lack the ability to criticize my own work, and even my best friends can't tell me. Your criticism was especially helpful. I am glad you rejected the short stories. I certainly don't want to publish inferior stuff."

Here was a man who used failure as a steppingstone to success.

Walt Disney is another example of this. It's amazing that the studio he founded is still a fantastic success almost forty years after his death. It's incredible that hundreds of millions of tourists continue to flock to Disneyland, Disney World, and the other Disney Magic Kingdoms around the world every year.

It becomes even more incredible when you realize that Walt Disney was wiped out financially in 1928. That was the year he naively signed away the rights to his successful animated character, Oswald the Lucky Rabbit. Oswald generated hundreds of thousands of dollars, but Walt didn't get a penny. If that had happened to me, I might have given up, gone home, and chosen another profession.

But Walt kept drawing. And in the meantime, he learned everything he could about business law. He wasn't about to be taken advantage of again. He learned from his mistakes. He used them to become strong in the places where he was weak. And in the shaky world of entertainment—where studios gain success on the basis of one hit and then disappear after one or two flops—Walt Disney Studios has been one of the giants for nearly seventy years.

I just finished writing a book on Walt Disney, titled *How to Be Like Walt*. In preparation for writing this book, I interviewed more than two hundred people who either knew him or who had researched his life. I also pored through seventy books in an effort to learn all I could about Walt Disney.

I discovered that it's almost a miracle that we've even heard of Walt Disney. He had absolutely no advantages to help him achieve success. He did not have a high-school diploma or a college degree. His parents were ordinary folks who had no great ambition for themselves or their children. He had no money and, in fact, went bankrupt twelve times. He had two nervous breakdowns.

There were times when everything seemed to be stacked against him. Yet he would not give up! In the end, Walt Disney became one of the most successful men in the world.

> SUCCESS GROWS OUT OF THE PROBLEMS YOU FACE HEAD-ON, NOT FROM THE PROBLEMS YOU AVOID.

Late in his life, Disney said, "I think it's important to have a good, hard failure when you're young. I learned a lot out of that, because it kind of makes you aware of what can happen to you. Because of it I've never had any fear in my whole life."

Walt Disney never wasted a moment. He used everything that happened to him in his movies, books, and other ventures.

I enjoy reading about successful people, and in doing so, I've discovered that Walt Disney's story is not unique. Most people who are considered to be great have overcome tremendous odds. They've come back again and again from failures that would have stopped lesser people. They have demonstrated the truth that success grows out of the problems you face head-on, and not from the problems you avoid.

A few years ago, my wife, Ruth, and I wrote a book called *How to Be Like Women of Influence*. We studied the lives of twenty great women and then did a summary of the characteristics they had in common. The number one trait, we found, was that they just would not quit, no matter what. Most of them had no one to cheer them on. They were going against popular opinion and ingrained sexual bigotry that held that women needed to know their place and stay in it. But they kept fighting against incredible odds, and they changed the world.

5. God's Strength Is Made Perfect in Our Weakness

A trial is an adverse circumstance that God either allows or brings into the lives of His children, in order to deepen their faith and commitment to Him. Trials are designed to make us grow, even though we may groan in the process.
TONY EVANS

I was channel-surfing in a hotel the other night (on another one of my speaking tours), and I came upon a TV evangelist talking about the importance of faith. Now, I agree that faith is terribly important. But in my opinion, this fellow had a distorted view of what it means to have faith. He said if you had proper faith, you would always be healthy, have plenty of money, drive a nice car, live in a great neighborhood, and never have any problems of any sort.

Yet when I read my Bible, I discover that Jesus said, "In this world you will have trouble. But take heart! I have overcome the world" (John 16:33). Jesus taught that trouble would be a natural part of life, even for those who belong to Him.

The apostle Paul was afflicted by something he referred to as "a thorn in my flesh" (2 Corinthians 12:7). We're not sure what it was, but he may have had trouble with his eyes. In his letter to the Galatians, he wrote, "I can testify that, if you could have done so, you would have torn out your eyes and given them to me" (Galatians 4:15).

Writing to the Christians in Corinth about his affliction, Paul says, "Three times I pleaded with the Lord to take it away from me. But he said to me, 'My grace is sufficient for you, for my power is made perfect in weakness.' Therefore I will boast all the more gladly about my weaknesses, so that Christ's power may rest on me. That is why, for Christ's sake, I delight in weaknesses, in insults, in hardships, in persecutions, in difficulties. For when I am weak, then I am strong" (2 Corinthians 12:8–10).

Author J. Oswald Sanders writes regarding Paul's thorn in the flesh: "At first he viewed it as a limiting handicap, but later he came to regard it as a heavenly advantage."

Never forget that some of the biggest heroes of the Bible were also failures:

- After insisting that he was ready to die for Jesus, the apostle Peter denied three times that he knew Christ. He also failed miserably in his attempt to walk on water—but then again, he was the only apostle with enough courage to try!

- King David committed adultery and then had his lover's

husband killed. You can't be much worse of a failure than that.

- Almost as soon as Noah got off the ark, he got rip-roaring drunk.

- Moses struck a rock with his staff so it would bring forth water, instead of merely speaking to it, as God had commanded.

- Abraham got into trouble twice because he lied and said that Sarah was his sister, instead of admitting that she was his wife. She was so beautiful he thought other men would kill him to take her away if they knew she was his wife.

- When God told Jonah to go preach to the people of Nineveh, he bought a ticket on a boat headed in the other direction.

- Mark, who wrote the Gospel bearing his name, deserted Paul and Barnabas after starting out on a missionary journey with them.

The Bible is full of stories about men and women who came back from failure to change the world for God. No matter where you've been or what you've done, I know you can do the same thing. I urge you to remember that, as Vince Lombardi said, "The real glory is in being knocked to your knees and then coming back."

Here's an important thing to keep in mind—if you belong

to God, anything that comes your way has to pass through a hedge of protection He has placed around you. That doesn't mean your life will be one long day at the beach, but you can have faith that "in all things God works for the good of those who love him, who have been called according to his purpose" (Romans 8:28).

Rest assured, that even includes your failures.

Building Block

Go the Extra Mile

Working hard overcomes a whole lot of other obstacles. You can have unbelievable intelligence, you can have connections, you can have opportunities fall out of the sky. But in the end, hard work is the true enduring characteristic of successful people.

Marsha Johnson

Far too many people have the attitude that the world owes them something. They have what a friend of mine calls "a sense of entitlement." And maybe it just seems this way because I'm getting older, but this attitude seems especially prevalent among today's younger generation.

When my Korean-born son Stephen was a graduate student at the University of Massachusetts, he had a five-week break over the Christmas and New Year's holidays. I didn't know that he had a long, detailed paper to write during that time.

I didn't know because I never saw him typing. He didn't do much of anything until four weeks had gone by. Then he was up against a near-impossible deadline.

I was angry and upset over his procrastination. "Stephen," I told him, "the world will run over you unless you get more aggressive and driven in life. You just can't do things this way!"

Stephen just waved his hands at me as if I didn't know what I was talking about.

"Light, Dad, light," he said, with a big smile on his face. "That's how I do it. Nice and light."

Unfortunately, "nice and light" doesn't get you very far on the road to success in life. But as my friend Bill Gaither said, "I am convinced that every child comes out of the womb looking for a shortcut." But there are no shortcuts. The only way to get what you want out of life is to work for it—and that means being willing to go the extra mile.

> THE ONLY WAY TO GET WHAT YOU WANT OUT OF LIFE IS TO WORK FOR IT—AND THAT MEANS BEING WILLING TO GO THE EXTRA MILE.

The phrase "go the extra mile" comes from Jesus's famous Sermon on the Mount, in which He said: "If someone forces you to go one mile, go with him two miles. Give to the one who asks you, and do not turn away from the one who wants to borrow from you" (Matthew 5:41–42).

For His contemporaries, Jesus's comment about going the extra mile had to be one of the most difficult of all His teachings. You see, in Jesus's day, all of Palestine was under Roman rule. According to the law, if you were not a Roman citizen, any of Caesar's soldiers had the right to stop you at any time and ask you to carry his equipment for a mile.

It didn't matter what you were doing. If a soldier beckoned you, you had to go. If you were working in your field, you dropped your hoe and went off to assist him. If you were on your way home from the market, you had to put your groceries down and go with the soldier. As far as Rome was concerned, you couldn't possibly be doing anything that was important enough to keep you from becoming a temporary armor bearer. Anyone who refused to go faced swift, severe punishment— even death.

Now, it wasn't easy carrying all that military equipment for a mile. It was heavy. Every soldier had his armor, his shield, his K rations, and who knows what else. By the time you got to the end of that mile, you were exhausted.

But the Romans considered themselves a civilized people (Nero notwithstanding). No soldier had the right to compel you to go with him for two miles. At the end of a mile, you were free to go, and he had to find someone else.

Yet Jesus said, in effect, "Do what they ask, and more. Show them God's love through your compassionate obedience. When you think you've done enough, you've really only gone halfway—so you've really got to put twice as much effort into everything you do."

In other words, do twice as much to please your parents. Do

twice as much for your children. Invest twice as much in your marriage and other relationships. Do double what your employer expects of you. If your music teacher expects you to practice the piano for one hour, practice for two hours. If you are required to spend an hour studying every evening, study for two hours, and so on.

Why should you do these things?

Because they will make you a better person.

Because you will learn more, do more, and be more.

When Jesus talked about going the extra mile, He wasn't just making an abstract statement that sounded good. He was telling us how God expects us to live.

I know it isn't easy to live this way. Christ expects a lot from His followers, but He also gives us the strength to do what He asks us to do. When Jesus says, "I want you to go the extra mile," and we ask why, He holds out his nail-scarred hands to show us how far He was willing to go for us. It's just not possible to argue with a Savior like that!

You can put our Lord's words into action by working as hard as you possibly can to get what you want out of life. There are no shortcuts. You can spend your entire life looking for Easy Street, but you'll never find it. My advice to every young person is, "Don't waste your time looking for the easy way to reach the finish line. Just roll up your sleeves and get to work."

Here are four important ways you can achieve success in life:

1. LEARN EVERYTHING YOU CAN ABOUT
   EVERYTHING YOU CAN.

2. WORK HARD NOW.

3. MAKE YOUR OWN LUCK.

4. REMEMBER THAT IT'S EASIER TO RUST OUT
   THAN IT IS TO WEAR OUT.

1. LEARN EVERYTHING YOU CAN ABOUT EVERYTHING YOU CAN

I will study and get ready,
and perhaps my chance will come.

ABRAHAM LINCOLN

A champion is someone with an insatiable curiosity and thirst for knowledge.

A champion stays well informed on current events by reading newspapers, magazines, and watching or listening to the news on television or radio.

Now, I know some Christians don't believe in paying attention to current events because they think it distracts their attention from God. However, God calls us to be the salt and light of the world (see Matthew 5:13–16), and we can't do that if we keep our heads stuck in the sand like an ostrich.

A champion knows the great works of literature. The philosopher Erasmus went so far as to say, "When I get a little money, I buy books; and if any is left I buy food and clothes." No, you can't read all of the world's best books. But you can and should read *some* of them.

I am grateful that my mother instilled in me a love for reading. There are few things I love more than a good book, and I read five or six a week. It's amazing the things you can learn by reading.

If you have difficulty finding the time to read, I suggest that you buy good books on tape or CD and listen to them in your car. That's a wonderful use of drive time. It can even turn an annoying traffic jam into something beneficial.

Where do you start? In a bookstore the other day, I saw a package of cards entitled *Fifty Great Works of Literature Everyone Should Read.* The package contained twenty-five cards, each side of which contained the title of a classic work of literature, a few lines about the author, and a brief synopsis of the book. What a great idea! Bear in mind, though, that anyone's list of classic literature is subjective. The books that appear on my list might not be on your list, and vice versa.

For example, one problem I had with this list of classics was that it didn't include any works by Christian authors such as G. K. Chesterton, C. S. Lewis, and J. R. R. Tolkien. In my opinion, these Christian classics should be very high on every champion's list of reading material.

A champion appreciates different styles of music. He doesn't limit himself to rock-'n'-roll, pop, rap, or country but learns to enjoy classical and opera as well. I recently discovered that one of my all-time great baseball heroes, Ted Williams, was a huge fan of classical music. He had a large record collection, was well versed on the styles of different composers, and often spent hours listening to music. That makes me respect him even more than I already did.

A champion strives to develop an appreciation and understanding of great art. Grant Hill is a great basketball player, and I'm thrilled that he wears the uniform of the Orlando Magic. He is a well-rounded individual who has a special interest in art and is considered to be an expert on the subject. He has even coauthored a book on art. Like all champions, Grant Hill has a wide range of interests and knowledge.

A champion learns from the wisdom and experiences of others. Champions are always growing and learning—from the day they are born until the day they die. They understand that, as educator Newton D. Baker said, "The man who graduates today, and stops learning tomorrow, is uneducated the day after."

2. Work Hard Now

Success usually comes to those who
are too busy to be looking for it.
Henry David Thoreau

"I will gladly pay you Tuesday for a hamburger today." If you watched cartoons when you were a kid, you surely recognize those words from Popeye's friend Wimpy.

Some people go through life always thinking that they'll get their act together "tomorrow."

"Hey! I'm young," they say. "I'll have plenty of time to work hard tomorrow. For now, I'm just going to take it easy and go with the flow."

The problem with that is that tomorrow never comes. All of a sudden, you're thirty-five or forty, and you find that you're far away from where you hoped you'd be at this point of your life.

I had the privilege of drafting Shaquille O'Neal out of Louisiana State University in 1992 and getting to know him during his years with the Orlando Magic. For my money, there has never been a more intimidating presence on a basketball court. But Shaq says that his career might never have achieved liftoff if not for his mother, who insisted that "there's no opportunity like now."

It's difficult for me to imagine that Shaq ever thought he couldn't be a star on the basketball court, but he says that was true. And because of his lack of confidence, he didn't feel like trying.

He writes, "I said, 'I can't do that right now. Maybe later.' Then my mother said the words that changed everything for me. She said, 'Later doesn't always come to everybody.' Those words snapped me into reality and gave me a plan. You work hard now. You don't wait. If you're lazy, or you sit back and don't want to excel, you'll get nothing. If you work hard enough, you'll be given what you deserve. Everything got easier for me after that."

A few years ago, I gave a speech in Minneapolis. After the event, a man came up and asked me if he could drive me to the airport to catch my flight back to Orlando. He seemed anxious to talk to me about something, so I said okay.

As we drove along, we made small talk for a few minutes, and then he told me what was on his mind. "It's about my son," he said.

I nodded and settled back in the seat, expecting to hear a tale of woe about a young man who was ruining his life with drugs and alcohol or reckless behavior.

"He's in the eighth grade," the fellow continued. "He's an excellent basketball player, and he loves the sport. He wants to play at the University of Minnesota."

"That's great!" I said. "Tell him I wish him well." It didn't sound like a difficult situation to me.

"Well, here's the problem: he wants to know right now that he's going to get a scholarship. Otherwise, he doesn't want to do all the work it's going to take for him to get to that level."

I wasn't quite sure what advice he wanted from me. All I could say was, "You'll have to tell your son that college coaches don't give scholarships to eighth-graders. If he wants a scholarship to the University of Minnesota, he'll have to prove himself in high school. That's just the way it is."

The dad nodded to let me know he heard me, and we drove on in silence. When I got home, I related the incident to my daughter Karyn, who was seventeen at the time, and asked her, "Is that how kids are thinking today? They want to know they're going to be rewarded before they're willing to do any work?"

She thought for a moment and said, "Yeah, Dad. I hate to tell you this, but that *is* how a lot of teenagers think."

Talk about putting the cart before the horse! There is only one way to achieve true success in life, and that is to work hard for it.

Russell Crowe didn't become a successful actor by telling a movie producer, "Give me ten million dollars to act in your movie, and I'll show you what I can do." He worked hard to perfect his craft. He proved that he had skill as an actor and the ability to do well at the box office. That's how he got to be one of the world's highest-paid and most sought-after actors.

> THERE IS ONLY ONE WAY TO ACHIEVE TRUE SUCCESS IN LIFE, AND THAT IS TO WORK HARD FOR IT.

Faith Hill didn't start out as a headliner, selling millions of albums and drawing thousands of fans to every concert. Like most singers, she started out working small clubs and opening for better-known acts. At one point, she even took a job stuffing envelopes for Reba McEntire's fan club. Hard work and talent combined to make her a star.

By the way, Faith Hill is married to country singer Tim McGraw, son of the late Tug McGraw, who became a friend of mine when we both lived in Philadelphia. Tug was pitching for the Phillies at the time, and I was general manager of the 76ers. I remember Tug telling me how happy he was that Tim had found a girl like Faith. He said, "She was very sweet, a great cook, and she could sing too. Little did we know she would become one of the best-known and best-selling singers in the world by being persistent in pursuit of her dream."

As it says on the sign hanging in the Cincinnati Reds' spring training clubhouse in Sarasota, Florida: "True champions are made when no one is looking."

3. Make Your Own Luck

Do not let what you cannot do
interfere with what you can do.
John Wooden

Some people seem to get all the good breaks. But they do that by putting themselves in the right position. They are like a Major League infielder who makes all the big plays.

A guy like Alex Rodriguez didn't become a great fielder just by luck. He knows all about the opposing batters. He knows what kind of pitch his pitcher is likely to throw in every situation. He's got a head full of statistics to go along with his athletic ability. He is constantly working to improve his knowledge of the game and to develop his skills as a baseball player. Then, when a bit of "luck" is needed in a pressure situation, he makes the impossible catch, stays with the difficult hop, or completes the amazing throw to nail the runner at first base.

Life is a lot like baseball. If you want to have good luck, you've got to keep your eyes open, be on your toes, and remain ready to react quickly when the situation warrants it. If you're not out there giving it your best, you're not putting yourself in a position where luck can find you.

As Gary Player, the great golfer from South Africa, once said, "The harder you work, the luckier you get."

Baseball great Ted Williams once said he believed there were hundreds of kids all over the country who had the ability to become great ballplayers but who would never make it to the top. Why not? Because, in Williams's words, "Nothing except practice, practice, practice will bring out that ability."

Hard work opens the doors for fortune to smile on you.

4. Remember That It's Easier to Rust Out Than It Is to Wear Out

Without work, people wither in the soul.
Ralph Wiley

When he died, the great violinist Niccolo Paganini left his violin to his hometown of Genoa, Italy. There was one stipulation: the violin was never again to be played.

Do you know what happened to that fine, well-crafted instrument? That's right: it decayed and became completely useless. In Paganini's hands, that violin had produced music that had thrilled audiences throughout Europe, but after his death it became a warped, worthless piece of wood.

A violin that is used properly—that is played regularly and kept in good repair—can last for hundreds of years and might even began to produce a richer, fuller tone over time. But left alone, it will crumble in its case, just as the great Paganini's violin did.

The same thing happens to a human being's skills and abilities. If we don't use them, they crumble and decay. God gave us specific talents because He expects us to develop them, and the only way we can develop them is by using them.

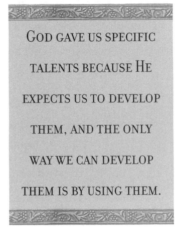

GOD GAVE US SPECIFIC TALENTS BECAUSE HE EXPECTS US TO DEVELOP THEM, AND THE ONLY WAY WE CAN DEVELOP THEM IS BY USING THEM.

A study undertaken by the Music Academy of West Berlin discovered that the best musicians were those who spent more time practicing. (No surprise there, right?) They didn't become superstars because they had more talent, but because they worked harder. In fact, by the time music students were eighteen, the best musicians had already spent about two thousand more hours in practice than those who were regarded as average in their musicianship.

In another study, a number of top achievers from the worlds of business, sports, music, and entertainment were asked to list the most important factors in their success. The most frequently mentioned factor, in every area, was hard work. It rated far higher than natural talent or ability.

You may not think of yourself as the swiftest arrow in the quiver. That may be true, but it doesn't really matter very much. If you try harder than the others, you'll go much further than they will! Hard work pays off—financially, spiritually, physically, mentally, and just about every other way you can think of.

I'd like to close this building block by reminding you of a few other ways that champions can go the extra mile:

Champions don't waste their time with thoughts about getting even, no matter what someone else may have done to them. They just keep moving forward, positively, all the time.

Champions refuse to get sidetracked by anger. Instead of nursing angry thoughts, champions vent their anger through physical exercise. (I mentioned before that doing something physical is the best way to work anger out of your system.)

Champions don't keep score. They don't say, "I did something good for her last time, so now it's time for her to do something good for me." Champions are willing to give and give and give some more, knowing that, "your Father, who sees what is done in secret, will reward you" (Matthew 6:4).

Champions don't make excuses. They don't look for reasons to quit. Theodore Roosevelt said, "Ninety percent of the work in this country is done by people who don't feel well." He may have been exaggerating, but his point is well taken. In sports, as in life, it is occasionally necessary to play through your pain. Champions understand that effort makes the difference between first place and commonplace.

Champions believe in possibilities, and not impossibilities. They understand that, as philosopher Elbert Hubbard said, "The world is moving so fast these days that the man who says it can't be done is generally interrupted by someone doing it."

Champions don't expect something for nothing. Michael Jordan put it this way: "I've always believed that if you put in the work, the results will come." Author Jack London said, "Don't loaf and invite inspiration. Take out after it with a club."

Work hard, do twice as much as others expect of you, and you will be a champion.

BUILDING BLOCK

NEVER GIVE UP

I hated every minute of the training, but I said, "Don't quit.
Suffer now, and live the rest of your life as a champion."
MUHAMMAD ALI

In 1996, when I was fifty-five years old, I ran in my first marathon—the Walt Disney Marathon in Orlando.

Don't ask me why I did it. I'm not sure.

Perhaps it was some sort of a midlife crisis. Maybe I just wanted to prove to myself that I *could* do it. But whatever the reason, I told my family and friends that I was going to compete in the 26.2-mile event, and then I started training for it.

I've always enjoyed running. And I've done my best to keep myself in shape.

Still, my friends thought I was crazy.

"You're not *really* going to run in the marathon, are you?" they'd ask.

"Yes, I am."

Usually, they'd just roll their eyes and walk away. They

probably figured my legs would turn to jelly about halfway through . . . that I'd wind up sprawled facedown on a sidewalk somewhere, and that would be the end of that.

But I did run in that marathon and was very pleased when I finished—and survived. I didn't set any world records. And the race was, for the most part, grueling and painful. But it is very difficult to describe the thrill and exhilaration I felt as I finally crossed the finish line. What a marvelous experience that was!

Since then, I've run in four to five long-distance races a year. In fact, I completed my thirty-third marathon in April 2005.

By the time I crossed the finish line, the Kenyan runners, as usual, had finished, showered, had their dinner, and were already halfway back home. That was okay with me, though, because I knew that I'd had a couple more hours than they did to enjoy the view along the route.

Even though I've been running in marathons for almost ten years, I still get the same question, "Why do you do it?" and the same incredulous looks. I understand that it's hard for people to see why running in marathons is so attractive to me. After all, running in a marathon beats your body to pieces.

From the time you're about five miles out, your body starts screaming to your brain that it's in pain and wants to quit: *What are we doing this for? We could be sitting by the swimming pool sipping on a nice, cold glass of lemonade! We've still got over twenty miles to go! No! You've got to be kidding!*

And marathons are expensive. There are entrance fees, and then there's the cost of travel, lodging, meals, and such. You do get a medal for finishing, but, realistically, the medal may be worth fifty cents. That's all.

So why do I do it?

Because it gives me a wonderful opportunity to practice "not quitting." And I know that this attitude of perseverance influences all other areas of my life. If I can keep on running to the finish line in a 26.2-mile race, then I have confidence that I can keep on running toward the goal in every other endeavor. And the payoff will be incredible.

If you want to be a champion in life, then no matter what happens to you, you've got to keep putting one foot in front of the other, heading directly toward your goal.

I love to read biographies about people who've helped to make the world a better place. I've read hundreds of them. And in almost every one, I've discovered there were plenty of times when the hero could have said, "That's it; I quit," but didn't. He or she kept on going no matter what, and eventually prevailed. Walt Disney called this attitude "stick-to-it-ivity." Whatever you call it, every champion has it.

Champions keep going because they believe in themselves and they believe in their goals. They don't listen to the naysayers—gloomy people who go around saying things like "It can't be done" and "You can't get there from here." (These are people like the ones who rejected Ronald Reagan when he auditioned to play the part of the president in a movie, saying that he "didn't look presidential.") Don't listen to people who are constantly critical.

Remember the childhood story of the little engine who pushed his way up the hill saying, "I think I can; I think I can"? Emulate that engine. Think positive thoughts. The majority of the time, if you think you can, you can. Don't quit!

Many years ago, actor Johnny Weissmuller—an Olympic swimming star who went on to play Tarzan in the movies—gave a pep talk to a group of aspiring actors. One of them asked, "What is the best advice you can give us?" Weissmuller smiled. "Don't let go of the vine."

When my daughter Karyn was a little girl, we enrolled her in gymnastics. For years, she was an eager and enthusiastic participant in the sport. Then, when she was about twelve, her attitude changed. She was tired of going to her classes and begged us to let her quit. We got so tired of hearing her complain that we finally gave in and said, "Okay. If you want to quit, quit." So she did.

Then, a few years later, when she was in high school, Karyn became a cheerleader. She discovered that, in order to do the best possible job, she needed to work on her gymnastics skills. So she reenrolled in the local program.

One day when I was driving her to class, she asked me, "Dad, why did you let me quit gymnastics?"

"Because you were moaning and groaning and making all our lives miserable," I teased her.

"Well," she said, "you should have made me stick with it. You shouldn't have let me quit, so don't let the other kids quit their stuff either."

I smiled as I realized that we had both learned an important lesson about refusing to quit.

Do you have a hard time persevering? Are you tempted to give up when trouble comes along? Do you start to think you can't possibly win?

Here are just a few of the good things that can happen to you if you have a never-quit attitude:

1. YOU CAN MAKE YOUR DREAMS COME TRUE.

2. YOU WILL BE AMAZED AT WHAT YOU CAN ACCOMPLISH.

3. YOU WILL BE A CONDUIT FOR THE INCREDIBLE POWER OF GOD.

4. YOU OPEN YOURSELF UP TO THE POSSIBILITY OF MIRACLES.

5. YOU WILL ACHIEVE GREATNESS.

Let's take a closer look at each of these benefits of perseverance.

1. YOU CAN MAKE YOUR DREAMS COME TRUE

Many men fail because they quit too soon. . . . If more of us would strike out and attempt to do the "impossible," we would find the truth of that old saying that nothing is impossible.
DR. C. E. WELCH

When a young black woman named Cora T. Walker told people she wanted to become an attorney, they laughed. Back in the 1940s, female lawyers were rare. Black lawyers were even rarer. And black female lawyers were practically nonexistent. Besides, Cora was growing up in a poor family in the middle of Harlem, New York. There wasn't a lot of money lying around to pay for law school. Her mother tried to talk some sense into her, but Cora wouldn't listen. She had a dream, and she had decided that she wasn't going to quit until she had achieved it.

Even after she sailed through college and was accepted into the law school at St. John's University, her dream still seemed unattainable. Her professor was open about his belief that women were not suited for law school. There were five females in the class, and he made it clear, right from the start, that he was going to make it tough on them.

He admitted that he believed Cora and the other women had come to school, not to get degrees in law, but because they were looking for husbands. He intended to do his best to get them to either flunk out or quit so he could give their spots on the roster to men, who really deserved them in the first place.

I'm not sure what happened to the other women in Cora's class. But I do know that Cora Walker earned her law degree in 1947. Even so, she still had a very hard time getting anyone to take her seriously. Several firms offered her a job as a legal secretary, but no one was willing to give her a chance as a lawyer.

Ever the risk taker, Cora opened her own office in Harlem and slowly built her own firm from the ground up. By the time she retired, Cora T. Walker was a millionaire many times over. Among her clients were Ford Motor Company and Texas Instruments. She is a shining example of what happens when you refuse to give up pursuit of your dream no matter how high the odds seem to be stacked against you.

2. You Will Be Amazed at What You Can Accomplish

The moment you commit and quit holding back, all sorts of unforeseen incidents, meetings, and material assistance will rise up to help you. The simple act of commitment is a powerful magnet for help.
Napoleon Hill

Dolly Parton has been a star in country music for more than thirty years. She's sold millions of records, starred in hit movies, and even has her own amusement park, Dollywood, in Tennessee. Recently, she opened a restaurant/entertainment center in my hometown of Orlando.

Dolly attended a very small high school in the mountains of Tennessee, and she remembers that, at a graduation event, all the seniors were invited to stand up and talk about their plans for the future.

One boy said he was going to college.

A girl said she was going to get married during the summer and move to a nearby town.

And so on.

But when it came Dolly's turn, she announced, "I'm going to Nashville to become a star." She was serious, but nobody else thought so.

"The entire place erupted in laughter," Dolly remembers. "I was stunned. Somehow, though, the laughter instilled in me an even greater determination to realize my dream."

Looking back on her successful career, Dolly Parton says there were many rough spots, many times when she was tempted to give up her dream and go home to the little mountain town she knew as a child. But whenever she was tempted to quit, she remembered the sound of laughter ringing in her ears, and it gave her the determination to go on.

Is Dolly Parton a talented singer and musician? Certainly. But there are talented people in every small town in America—and we've never heard of most of them. It was determination and perseverance, more than any other qualities, that made Dolly Parton a star.

When he was the top-ranked tennis player in the world, Bjorn Borg gave this reason for his success: "My greatest point is my persistence. I never give up in a match. However down I am,

I fight until the last ball. My list of matches shows that I have turned a great many so-called irretrievable defeats into victories." Nearly one hundred years earlier, boxing champion James J. Corbett said, "You become a champion by fighting one more round. When things are tough, you fight one more round."

What was true one hundred years ago is still true today.

3. YOU WILL BE A CONDUIT FOR THE INCREDIBLE POWER OF GOD

Let us throw off everything that hinders and the sin that so easily entangles, and let us run with perseverance the race marked out for us. Let us fix our eyes on Jesus, the author and perfecter of our faith, who for the joy set before him endured the cross, scorning its shame, and sat down at the right hand of the throne of God.
HEBREWS 12:1–2

Imagine how Moses must have felt.

In front of him, the Red Sea stretched out as far as he could see. Behind him, Egyptian charioteers, armed to the teeth, were bearing down on him. Between Moses and those Egyptian soldiers stood hundreds of thousands of Israelites, most of them screaming in terror, all of them looking to Moses to save them.

I wonder if, just for a moment, Moses thought maybe he'd been the victim of some cosmic practical joke. Had God brought the children of Israel out of captivity in Egypt just to destroy them? If ever a man was tempted to just give up, it must have been Moses on that scary day.

But if you'll pick up your Bible and read that story, in the fourteenth chapter of Exodus, you'll find that Moses didn't quit. God said to him, "Tell the Israelites to move on," and that's what he did (Exodus 14:15). Then the Bible tells us that "the LORD drove the sea back with a strong east wind and turned it

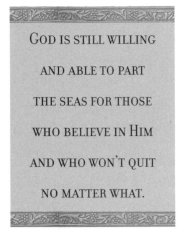

GOD IS STILL WILLING
AND ABLE TO PART
THE SEAS FOR THOSE
WHO BELIEVE IN HIM
AND WHO WON'T QUIT
NO MATTER WHAT.

into dry land. The waters were divided, and the Israelites went through the sea on dry ground, with a wall of water on their right and on their left" (verses 21–22). When the Egyptians tried to pursue them, the waters came back together and drowned them all.

I believe that God is still willing and able to part the seas for those who believe in Him and who won't quit no matter what obstacles might be facing them.

Pastor and author Chuck Swindoll asks this question: "Are you facing some difficult battle today? If you are, He says: "Don't run! Stand still . . . and refuse to retreat. Look at it as God looks at it and draw upon His power to hold up under the blast. Sure, it's tough. Nobody ever said the Christian life was easy."

We've talked before about the fact that success in life—as the world sees success—is not necessarily a sign of God's blessing. You can get yourself into big trouble by thinking, *My life is going well—so God must be pleased with me.* That's the kind of thinking that led to the downfall of televangelist Jim Bakker— who served a prison term for fraud. It seemed that no matter what Bakker did, donations continued to pour into his PTL television network. Surely, if God was unhappy with him, the money would stop coming in—wouldn't it?

Not necessarily. The Bible says that Satan can transform himself into an "angel of light" (2 Corinthians 11:14). He can make you think you're sailing along toward the goal when you're really just going around in circles. Often, when things are going well, people don't recognize their need for God.

When difficulties come along, we're most likely to reach out for God, and He is most likely to make His presence known to us. The Old Testament book of Daniel tells the story of three men who were thrown into a furnace because they refused to bow down to an idol erected by King Nebuchadnezzar. After the three men were bound and thrown into the furnace, the Bible says that King Nebuchadnezzar leaped to his feet in amazement and said, "Look! I see four men walking around in the fire, unbound and unharmed, and the fourth looks like a son of the gods" (Daniel 3:25).

Immediately, the king called for the three men to come out of the furnace. The king's awe was increased when he discovered that their hair was not even singed and their clothing did not smell like smoke.

It is usually in the "furnaces" of life that God's presence and power are made known to His people. In fact, I think He sometimes allows us to get into trouble, just because He wants us to know that we can trust Him in any situation. Our job is to keep on going no matter what obstacles may be in our way.

4. YOU OPEN YOURSELF UP TO THE POSSIBILITY OF MIRACLES

Life has two rules: Number one, never quit;
number two, always remember rule number one.
DUKE ELLINGTON

Perhaps you have heard of the miracle of the bamboo tree that grows in Malaysia. It serves as a terrific reminder of the importance of perseverance.

The first year after he plants the bamboo, the Malaysian farmer waters, fertilizes, and cultivates his crop.

Nothing happens.

The next year, he carefully waters, fertilizes, and cultivates again.

Nothing happens.

The third year? You guessed it. More water and more fertilizer.

But again, nothing happens. I don't know about you, but I think I'd decide to give up right about then. The farmer has absolutely nothing to show for three years of hard work.

Yet he goes out for a fourth year and does it again.

With the same results. Or, perhaps I should say the same lack of results.

Undaunted, as the fifth anniversary of the planting rolls around, he goes back out and starts the routine all over again.

And in the next thirty days, the bamboo shoots ninety feet into the sky. That's not a misprint. Not nine feet or ninety inches, but ninety feet—the height of a nine-story building.

You see, you just never know what's going to happen if you refuse to give up.

Dr. Frank Minirth, one of the founders of the Minirth-Meier Clinic, tells a wonderful story about the brilliant Polish pianist Jan Paderewski.

Just before one of his concerts was about to begin, as the master was preparing to make his entrance, a small boy of perhaps five or six climbed up onto the stage, sat down at the piano, and began playing a clumsy version of "Chopsticks." The audience was shocked by the child's behavior and began to boo loudly. A man shouted, "Somebody stop him!" Someone else yelled, "Get that boy off the stage!"

> IT IS USUALLY IN THE "FURNACES" OF LIFE THAT GOD'S PRESENCE AND POWER ARE MADE KNOWN TO HIS PEOPLE.

Backstage, Paderewski heard the commotion, grabbed his coat, and rushed onto the stage. Instead of shooing the child away from the piano, he bent over the boy and began playing improvised music that beautifully complemented the boy's childish "plunking." As he played,

Paderewski whispered, "Keep playing, son. Don't quit. Keep playing."

When the duet was finished, the audience erupted into deafening applause. They believed that the song had been planned as an innovative way to begin the concert. But it hadn't been planned at all. It was the master's grace and skill that had turned the boy's stumbling performance into a thing of beauty.

Dr. Minirth said, "That is, in essence, what God promises to do with our errors, failures, and distresses. He will play around them until they sound better. When we sit down in heaven, there will be thunderous applause."

5. YOU WILL ACHIEVE GREATNESS

I'm not so smart. It's just that I stay with problems longer.
ALBERT EINSTEIN

According to a study done by the Tulane University School of Business, the average entrepreneur fails 3.8 times before he or she finally succeeds. It's not necessarily true that "the third time is the charm." It may be the fourth, fifth, sixth . . . or twenty-sixth attempt that finally pays off. The only way you can ever get to the finish line is to keep on keeping on.

I recently came across these amazing statistics about people who were willing to persevere to achieve their goals:

- Ernest Hemingway went back through his manuscript of *The Old Man and the Sea* eighty times, editing, rewriting, and smoothing the text.

- Sir Walter Scott put in fifteen hours every day at his desk, rising at four in the morning to write. He averaged a new book every two months.

- Plato rewrote the first sentence of *The Republic* nine times before he finally got it the way he wanted it.

- Virgil spent twelve years working on the *Aeneid*, and he was still perfecting the manuscript at the time of his death.

- Leonardo da Vinci worked on *The Last Supper* for ten years, sometimes becoming so absorbed in his work that he'd forget to eat.

- More than two thousand preliminary sketches of Michelangelo's *The Last Judgment* were found among his papers after his death.

Pay careful attention to these wise words from Chuck Swindoll: "The thing that makes for greatness is determination, persisting in the right direction over the long haul, following your dream, staying at the task. Just as there is no such thing as instant failure, neither is there automatic or instant success. But success is the direct result of a process that is long, arduous, and often unappreciated by others. It also includes a willingness to sacrifice. But it pays off if you stay at the task."

On the prairies of northern Montana in the late 1880s, a farmer was headed home from his fields when a blizzard blew in. The snow was coming down so fast that he quickly became completely disoriented. He walked through the blizzard for hours, looking in vain for a lantern shining in a window or some other sign that he was nearing safety and shelter.

Tragically, he never found what he was looking for.

Finally, exhausted and discouraged, he gave up. He lay down in the snow, curled up in an effort to keep warm, and went to sleep.

That's where they found his body the next morning—less than fifteen feet from his front door. Just a few more steps through the snow, and he would have been safe.

Never give up! You can never know when the moment of victory and triumph—the moment you've been waiting for—is going to come.

REMEMBER THAT CHARACTER COUNTS

Character embodies all of who you truly are. It is the inner fiber of your being. It is your inner self in action. It reveals what you are truly made of. It's your substance.
JOHN MAXWELL

If you want to be a champion, you must be a person of honesty *and* integrity.

Honesty means that everything you say is true—that people can count on your word. Integrity implies completeness, wholeness.

A person of integrity has no chinks in his or her armor. He does not wear a mask. She's genuine. He or she treats everyone with the same respect and courtesy. As you strive to be a person of integrity in every situation, you will build character that will help you achieve lasting success in life.

I do a weekly radio show in Orlando. When I interviewed Whitey Herzog, former Major League manager, I asked him his greatest strength as a manager. He replied, "I was always honest with my players. They knew they could talk to me at any time and I'd never lie to them. That built up the trust they had in me."

A few years ago, I got a call from a man named Pat Thomas, who told me this story. He had been at his tennis club about 6 p.m. the previous day and had set his briefcase on the back of his car. When his tennis game was over, he got into the car and drove off, forgetting all about the briefcase, which contained a number of important business papers—plus his wallet full of credit cards, his driver's license, and about thirty dollars in cash.

He told me that several other drivers honked and pointed at him as he was driving home—but for some reason, he just didn't make the connection. His car seemed to be running fine. It didn't feel like a tire was going flat. So he just kept going.

It wasn't until he pulled into his driveway that he remembered where he'd left the briefcase. That's when the panic set in. He was just walking out the door, planning to retrace his steps in the hope of finding it somewhere along the way, when his phone rang.

The caller was our house manager, Angel Garcia, who had seen the briefcase lying in the middle of the highway and stopped to pick it up. "Where can I meet you to give it back to you?" he asked.

Overjoyed, Mr. Thomas said he'd come right away. When he met Angel, he offered to give him a financial reward, but Angel said no. He told Mr. Thomas that he was returning the briefcase simply because he was a Christian who wanted to do the right thing, and not because he wanted a reward.

Mr. Thomas wasn't willing to take no for an answer. "Why don't I just give you a reward and you can give it to your favorite charity?"

Again, Angel said no. "I work for Pat Williams," he said, "and I know he wouldn't want me to take your money."

Mr. Thomas called me just to let me know that Angel's good character had impressed him. "He could have just left my briefcase lying there in the road, but he wouldn't do that. He could have just taken the money out of my wallet and thrown everything else away. But he wouldn't do that either.

"I want you to know," he told me, "that you have a really good guy working for you. I wish there were more people like him."

I hung up the phone thinking about how much better our society would be if everyone had Angel's character. Wouldn't it be great if everybody behaved honestly, even when nobody was looking?

That's what it means to have character. Character is what you do when you know you can get away with anything.

Here's the way I said it in my book *American Scandal*:

It is almost impossible to overestimate the importance of character. I would go so far as to say that an absence of character is responsible for most of the disasters that have befallen the human race. Man's inhumanity to man—the result of a lack of character—has caused more suffering and pain than all of the national disasters that have occurred since this planet was created! . . .

On the other hand, character in a time of crisis can avert disaster and help to build a brighter, better tomorrow.

Here are a few of the most important ingredients that go into making up a person of high moral character:

1. *C*OMMITMENT

2. *H*ONOR

3. *A*TTITUDE

4. *R*ESPONSIBILITY

5. *A*BSTINENCE

6. *C*OURAGE

7. *T*RUTHFULNESS

8. *E*THICS

9. *R*EPUTATION

1. Commitment

*There are always temptations, but you show true strength as
a man when you say no to temptation. You turn your back
on the temporary five minutes of gratification or five minutes
of happiness and you can experience the joy of Christ.*

Mike Sweeney

A person of character is loyal to his friends, his family, his employer, and, most especially, to his God.

He is not fickle. He won't desert you when you're outnumbered or let you down when you need a shoulder to cry on. He is an example of what the Bible means when it says, "A friend loves at all times" (Proverbs 17:17).

The motto for the United States Marine Corps is *semper fidelis*. That is Latin for "always faithful," and it's a wonderful description of people who demonstrate the character trait of commitment.

I recently read a newspaper article about a female private detective who makes a great deal of money from other women who hire her to find out if their husbands or boyfriends can be trusted. She flirts with the men, and if they take the bait, she reports back that the guy can't be trusted and that the marriage, or relationship, should be ended. She said that very few men turn down her advances.

It's distressing that so many men are willing to throw away an important relationship—and even a marriage—for a few minutes of pleasure. It's like exchanging a diamond worth one million dollars for a zirconium ring that costs less than ten bucks at Wal-Mart! It makes no sense.

Champions commit themselves to things that are really important in life, and they hold on to them no matter what.

Do you remember the fable about the dog that was carrying a big bone across a bridge that passed over a tranquil lake? The mutt looked down into the lake's surface and saw his own reflection—but he thought he was looking at another dog carrying a bone. What's more, the other dog's bone looked bigger and tastier than the one *he* had.

In fact, it looked so big and so tasty that he felt he just had to have it, so he tried to grab it. When he did, he got nothing but a snoot full of water, and his own bone fell into the lake and quickly disappeared beneath the surface.

That illustrates what happens to people who confuse flash with substance. They find out that there was no substance behind the flash, and they wind up losing everything of value.

Champions do not break their commitments. They do not turn back on their promises. And, because they don't, they are generally content and happy.

2. HONOR

Honor is better than honors.
ABRAHAM LINCOLN

You don't hear a great deal about honor these days. It's kind of an old-fashioned word, like *chivalry*.

Yet personal honor is every bit as important as it was two hundred years ago. And if the world is still here two hundred years from now, it will be just as important then.

What is honor? It is striving to do the right thing in every situation.

Honor is always going by the rules, even when everyone else around you is taking shortcuts and cheating.

Honor is seeking to build up rather than tear down.

Honor is being quick to admit your mistakes and to apologize for them.

Honor is being considerate of other people's feelings.

Honor is being trustworthy at all times.

Honor is typified by the men and women who are serving this country in Iraq and other trouble spots around the world— people who have put other people's welfare ahead of their own safety. And honor was exemplified by the firefighters and policemen who rushed into the World Trade Center on 9/11 as everyone else was scrambling to get out.

I have a friend who prays every day, "Lord, help me to behave in such a way today that You will be proud of me." That's a great prayer for anyone who wants to be known as a person of honor.

Always act honorably, and you will have few regrets in life.

3. Attitude

Weakness of attitude becomes weakness of character.
Albert Einstein

It's important to:

Believe in yourself.

Expect the best from others.

See the glass as half full instead of half empty.

Trust in God.

In other words, strive to have the BEST possible attitude about everything that happens to you.

During the holiday season last year, I overheard a woman telling her friend about the ordeal she went through trying to get a Christmas tree home from the tree lot. She was a couple of miles from home, she said, when she turned a corner and the tree slid off the top of her car.

"How awful!" her friend gasped. "You must have been furious."

The first woman chuckled. "Actually, it was hilarious," she said. "I couldn't stop laughing. I'd never laughed so hard in my life."

"It's a good thing it didn't happen to me," her friend replied. "I sure wouldn't have been laughing."

You want to know something? Neither would I.

But I'm trying to get to the place where I *would* laugh at something like that. It would be great to have an attitude that takes life's daily setbacks in stride and finds some joy and even humor in them.

Someone might say, "But some people are just happy by nature. I can't help it if I have a melancholy personality." While that may be true to a degree, I believe anyone can develop a better, more positive attitude simply by practicing seeing things in a positive light. Although it may sound simplistic, one of the very best things you can do is put a smile on your face. You may not mean it at first. But if you keep smiling, after a while, you *will* mean it. Your outlook will brighten, and things will just seem better than before.

Before we leave the subject of attitude, I want to mention that it is extremely important to learn to trust in God. He does know what's best for you, and you can trust Him even when you're out in a tiny little boat in the middle of a huge storm (see Mark 4:35–41).

Here's a promise you can hang on to when the going gets a bit tough: "We know that in all things God works for the good of those who love him, who have been called according to his purpose" (Romans 8:28).

4. Responsibility

Everybody complains about the weather,
but nobody does anything about it.
Mark Twain

Of course, the joke is that nobody *can* do anything about the weather. But in our day, a lot of people go around complaining about things they could do something about, if they'd only try. For example:

A fellow complains about the way the local school system is being run, but he refuses to consider running for a seat on the school board.

A woman complains to her neighbor about potholes on their street, but she won't take the time to go to a city council meeting to ask to have them filled.

Someone else gripes about kids hanging out on the streets and being unsupervised after school, but he doesn't volunteer to help out at the tutoring center, be a Scout leader, or get involved in a junior sports program.

My point is that it's easy to complain, but champions go a step further to do something about those problem areas. They realize that we are all responsible for the quality of life.

I'm sorry to say that some people don't take responsibility for anything—even themselves. They have an excuse for every situation. They say, "You can't expect me to do any better in life. After all, I come from a poor family . . . was mistreated by my parents . . . am disabled . . . am a member of a minority race . . . have a learning disability . . . am overweight . . ." And on and on.

When it gets right down to it, just about everyone can find a reason why they are not really responsible and are destined for failure.

A champion takes responsibility anyway and succeeds.

5. ABSTINENCE

*Dear friends, I urge you . . . to abstain from
sinful desires, which war against your soul.*
1 PETER 2:11

When most people see the word *abstinence,* they think of sex. While I believe that sex outside of marriage is wrong, I also believe there are other important areas where abstinence is important.

Champions abstain from tobacco, because they know it can kill them. If our lungs were on the outside, where we could actually see them, no one would smoke. I recently came across this statement by Dr. John Tickell and thought it was important enough to pass along: "You smoke? You're kidding me. The stuff that comes out the back end of a cigarette is basically the same stuff that comes out the back end of an automobile. Carbon monoxide, hydrogen cyanide—they are lethal poisons. And people worry about chemical threats!"

Champions abstain from alcohol, because they know it can impair their judgment and cause them to behave unwisely. During the 2003 football season, former New York Jets quarterback Joe Namath got some negative publicity because of an embarrassing interview at halftime of a game broadcast by ESPN. Namath's speech was slurred, and he twice told the interviewer that he wanted to kiss her. Later, upon announcing that he was getting involved in a rehab program, Namath said, "Every time something in my life has gone awry, alcohol has been involved." His are profound words worth heeding.

Champions abstain from illegal drugs and misuse of prescription drugs, because they know that drugs can dull their senses, take them captive, and prevent them from fulfilling the potential God placed within them.

Champions abstain from gambling. Gambling can be just as

addictive and just as dangerous as anything else we've mentioned. Whether it's playing the lottery or betting on football games, any kind of gambling can quickly dominate your life and leave you with tremendous debts you can't possibly pay. Gambling truly is a life-threatening activity.

Champions abstain from the very appearance of evil. As the Bible says, "Avoid every kind of evil" (1 Thessalonians 5:22).

How do you know if something is evil and should be avoided? Here's a good rule of thumb: *if it gives you a guilty conscience, don't do it.*

6. COURAGE

Courage is the ladder on which all other virtues mount.
CLARE BOOTHE LUCE

In his book *The Screwtape Letters,* C. S. Lewis wrote, "Courage is not simply one of the virtues, but the form of every virtue at the testing point."

It takes courage not to turn your back on a commitment when the going gets tough.

It takes courage not to tell a lie when the truth might get you into trouble.

It takes courage to admit you're responsible when it would be easy to place the blame on others.

It takes courage to say no to your friends when you know they might laugh at you.

It takes courage just to make the right decisions as you go through life from day to day.

As Chuck Swindoll wrote, "Courage is not limited to the battlefield or the Indianapolis 500 or bravely catching a thief in your house. The real tests of courage are much quieter. They are the inner tests: remaining faithful when nobody's looking; enduring pain when the room is empty; standing alone when you're misunderstood."

IT TAKES REAL COURAGE TO QUIETLY AND DETERMINEDLY DO THE RIGHT THING.

When my son Stephen was seventeen years old, I drove him to Tallahassee to start his college career at Florida State University. I took him out to dinner, then I drove him back to his dorm, told him good-bye, and headed out on the four-hour drive back to Orlando.

As I drove away, I watched in the rearview mirror as he waved good-bye, and I felt a huge lump forming in my throat. This was going to be the first time Stephen had spent more than a few days away from home since we had adopted him and his twin brother, Thomas, and brought them from Korea when they were very little boys.

As Stephen disappeared from view, I began to pray, "Lord, please give him courage. Help him do the right thing. Help him to resist the pressure when the other guys in the dorm want him to do something he knows he shouldn't do. Help him say yes when he needs to say yes, and to say no when he needs to say no."

You see, to me it takes real courage to quietly and determinedly do the right thing. I am pleased that God gave Stephen the courage to stand up for his beliefs.

Jesus Christ is the greatest example of courage who ever lived. He was courageous because He spoke out for what was right, even though His message was at odds with the religious and government leaders of the day. He was courageous because He reached out in love to the poor and dispossessed—to tax collectors, prostitutes, and other notorious sinners—thereby causing people to call him "a glutton and a drunkard" (Matthew 11:19).

But the primary way Jesus showed His courage was by going into Jerusalem to give Himself up to those who wanted to kill Him. Jesus knew He was going to be tortured and murdered in Jerusalem, but He also knew that His death was central to God's plan for man's redemption from sin. Even though His disciples urged Him not to go into the city, the Bible tells us that Jesus "resolutely set out for Jerusalem" (Luke 9:51).

Since our Lord showed so much courage on our behalf, we also ought to be courageous for Him.

7. TRUTHFULNESS
Your integrity will affect your destiny.
Don't leave home without it.
CLARENCE E. HODGES

Stephen Covey, author of *The 7 Habits of Highly Effective People*, was once asked how a person can build character. He replied,

"Make a promise, and keep it. Then make another promise, and keep that one too." In other words, be truthful. Do what you say you're going to do. Don't make promises you do not have the ability, or the intention, of keeping. Be honest.

Someone has said, "If you tell one lie, you're a liar." That statement is harsh, perhaps—but it's true. As author Awson O'Malley said, "Those who think it is permissible to tell 'white lies' soon grow colorblind."

I recently read a story about a silver-tongued attorney who was trying to get his client acquitted on a murder charge. All the evidence seemed to point toward the suspect's guilt—yet the main point in his favor was that the alleged victim's body had not been found.

In his final arguments, the defense attorney made an astounding announcement.

"Ladies and gentleman of the jury," he said, "my client is totally innocent of the charges against him. There has been no murder. In fact, the alleged victim is here today and is about to come walking through those doors."

A gasp was heard as the attorney pointed toward the back of the courtroom. Every head turned in the direction of those doors.

One minute passed . . . and then another . . . but nobody entered the courtroom.

The attorney then addressed the jury again: "I apologize for telling you something that obviously did not come true;

however, the mere fact that you looked at the doors as you did showed me, and shows you, that you have some measure of doubt. And, of course, if you have any doubt at all, you must return a verdict of 'not guilty.'"

He returned to his seat, obviously pleased with himself, as the jury filed out to deliberate. Fewer than fifteen minutes later, they were back with a verdict.

The foreman stood up, faced the judge, and said, "Your Honor, we find the defendant guilty of first-degree murder."

The attorney was outraged. "How could you? I saw all of you watching that door!"

"Yes, sir," the jury foreman admitted. "We were watching that door—but we were also watching you and your client. You didn't look at the door, and neither did he. You both knew there wasn't a chance in the world that anyone was going to walk into this courtroom."

You see, even the cleverest lies will be found out.

Make up your mind, in advance, that you will tell the truth in every situation. The truth may not always be easy. It may have some difficult circumstances attached to it. Even so, the adage is true: honesty really is the best policy.

8. ETHICS

Live in such a way that you would not be ashamed
to sell your parrot to the town gossip.
WILL ROGERS

A champion doesn't have to spend a lot of time wondering if the decisions he's making are right or wrong, morally. He has a well-developed sense of values that guide him in nearly every situation. These are his ethics.

Champions have made up their minds in advance that it's not okay to tell a lie, cheat on a test, pad their résumés, climb the ladder by backstabbing other people, or to keep the extra ten dollars when the clerk undercharges them. They are guided by their inner principles, even in the most difficult or trying circumstances.

Here's some good advice from Jesus Christ: "In everything, do to others what you would have them do to you" (Matthew 7:12).

Jesus also said, "'Love the Lord your God with all your heart and with all your soul and with all your mind.' This is the first and greatest commandment. And the second is like it: 'Love your neighbor as yourself'" (Matthew 22:37–39).

If you love God, you'll try not to do anything that breaks His heart. And if you love your neighbor, you won't want to do anything that breaks his or her heart.

An ethical person has certain questions that he asks himself before making any difficult decision:

- Will this please God?

- Will it hurt someone?

- Would I want someone else to do to me what I'm about to do?

- If my parents (or my spouse or my children) knew what I'm about to do, would they be proud of me—or would they feel embarrassed and ashamed?

- How would I feel if I knew that tomorrow morning's newspaper was going to carry an article on what I'm about to do?

- What would happen if everyone made decisions like this one?

Champions ask themselves these questions and always make ethical decisions, no matter the consequences.

9. REPUTATION

Ultimately, all you will have left at the end of the day are your name and your reputation. Invest in them wisely, and you and others will simultaneously reap the rewards.

LEONARD SCHLESINGER

Having a good reputation is important for everyone.

Even God.

The third of the Ten Commandments is: "You shall not misuse the name of the LORD your God" (Exodus 20:7).

Most of us have come to think that this commandment is talking about swearing, but that's only part of the picture. God is also warning us not to smudge His reputation. In other words, don't say you belong to God and then go out and lie, cheat, or steal.

In Old Testament times, Jewish businessmen would often

complete a business deal by swearing on the name of Yahweh. That meant the contract was binding. There was no need to have your attorney draw up a twenty-five-page contract. Just swear on God's name and that was enough.

In the third commandment, God is saying, "If you swear something in My name, then you'd better do it. You'd better take me seriously. You'd better not damage My reputation."

Why should God worry about His reputation? Because He wants His followers to draw other people to Him, not drive them away. If someone is able to look at you and say, "That guy calls himself a Christian, but he acts like a total jerk," then that person isn't likely to be drawn to Christ.

When Christians are meanspirited, selfish, and rude, they reflect poorly on the name of Christ. In effect, they damage the Lord's reputation.

A champion recognizes that his or her reputation is important because it not only reflects upon him, but upon his family, his career, and his God. A champion isn't one of those people who says, "I couldn't care less what people think about me." He understands that some people are going to think the worst of you no matter what you do. He knows that even the best people are sometimes going to be the subject of vicious rumors and gossip. But he also understands that, for the most part, a good reputation is built by good behavior.

Why do so many Americans shop for name brands, when

other products cost less? It's because the companies that manufacture those name brands have built their reputations through years of providing quality products and services. I've never heard anybody say, "Oh, I bought this suit from the Brand-X company because they have a reputation for making shoddy merchandise." In business, and in life, a good reputation can take you far.

The Bible says, "A good name is more desirable than great riches; to be esteemed is better than silver or gold" (Proverbs 22:1).

LIVE BY THE FAITH PHENOMENON

We live by faith, not by sight.
2 CORINTHIANS 5:7

It's amazing how much we do by faith.

We have faith that a chair is strong enough for us to sit in it.

We have faith that the sun will come up in the morning and that it will go down at night.

We board an airplane and have faith that it's going to fly us to our next destination. Nobody calls the airline and says, "I'd like one chance on your next flight to New York."

While it is important to have faith in things like chairs and airplanes and such, it is much more important to have faith in God.

I've spent a lot of time in this book talking about the importance of having a proper relationship with God, but I'm bringing it up again because it's so vital.

In Jesus Christ, God came to earth in human form. Because

of what Christ experienced, God knows how we feel when we're facing difficult times and situations (see Hebrews 4:15). I hope this doesn't sound irreverent, but I believe that Jesus knows what it feels like to have a big, ugly zit on the tip of your nose. He knows what it's like to get picked on by the older kids. (I'm quite sure there were bullies two thousand years ago, just as there were bullies when I was a kid, and there are bullies today.) Jesus knows what it feels like to be cold, tired, unable to sleep because of a toothache, or to have an upset stomach or a headache. You name the pain or embarrassment, and He's felt it.

Christian churches are full of people who can attest to the fact that their lives have been changed forever through an encounter with the risen Lord. He is touching people and changing lives just as He did when He walked the dusty roads of Judea two thousand years ago.

Champions choose to have faith in Jesus Christ, and they experience the incredible difference that faith makes in life. When you live by the faith phenomenon, here are a few of the incredible things you will discover:

1. GIVING YOUR LIFE TO CHRIST WILL CHANGE EVERYTHING.

2. LIVING BY FAITH IS AN EXCITING ADVENTURE.

3. You are secure in God at all times.

4. God will never leave you.

1. Giving Your Life to Christ Will Change Everything

I know one hall of fame I'll always be a part of is God's hall of fame. Jesus has been in my heart my whole career, and He needs to be given the praise that He deserves.
Gary Carter

Jesus said, "Anyone who has seen me has seen the Father" (John 14:9). True champions recognize their need for God and come to Him by accepting the gift of salvation that comes through faith in Christ.

After I recently spoke on the topic of faith, a woman told me about something that happened when she was a little girl, living in Wadesboro, North Carolina. "My grandmother had a lot of physical ailments," she told me, "but her doctor couldn't speak English. He would write out the prescription in Latin—then she'd take it to the pharmacist, who would translate it and give her what she needed."

"Your grandmother had a lot of faith to take that medicine," I laughed.

"She sure did," the woman replied. "And I figure that if my grandmother could trust those two men with her life, I can most certainly trust God with mine."

Amen! Faith can make all the difference in a person's life. John 3:16 speaks of the importance of faith: "For God so loved the world that he gave his one and only Son, that whoever believes in him shall not perish but have eternal life." Then there's the thirty-sixth verse of the same chapter: "Whoever believes in the Son has eternal life, but whoever rejects the Son will not see life, for God's wrath remains on him."

> ACCEPTING CHRIST AS YOUR SAVIOR IS JUST THE BEGINNING OF THE MOST AMAZING, INCREDIBLE, EXCITING LIFE ANYONE COULD EVER EXPERIENCE.

Jesus also said, "I am the way and the truth and the life. No one comes to the Father except through me" (John 14:6).

After His resurrection, Jesus told His disciples, "Go into all the world and preach the good news to all creation. Whoever believes and is baptized will be saved, but whoever does not believe will be condemned" (Mark 16:15–16).

If you've been thinking about becoming a Christian but haven't yet made up your mind to turn your life over to Christ, go back to the introduction of this book and reread what I wrote about building your life on the foundation of Jesus Christ.

Writer Fred Smith, now eighty-nine years old, looks back on a long life of service to Christ. He recently shared an incident from many years ago that had a profound effect on him. Smith, who was selling life insurance at the time, made a business call on a man who demanded to know, "What is your blood type?"

Fred wrote, "When I told him, he said, 'That is exactly what we need.' And then he said, 'My brother is dying in St. Thomas Hospital and must have blood immediately. Will you give him some?' I was happy to oblige. We immediately got in the car and went out." At the hospital, he remembers, "I lay down on a cot—a mobile cot—beside him, and they transferred the blood directly from me to him because it was that urgent."

Smith adds, "He lived and was very grateful for the transfusion, and he once mentioned that he would be happy to pay me. But he saw that his gratitude was enough and financial payment would be inappropriate. I have never seen him again, but the experience has produced total satisfaction."

Why did Fred Smith share this experience? Because it taught him something very important: "When our souls were perishing, Christ provided a way for salvation and eternal life. Christ gave us something that we cannot buy—we can only receive it by faith—it came from his grace."

Accepting Christ as your Savior isn't where the adventure ends. That is just the beginning of the most amazing, incredible, exciting life anyone could ever experience.

My wife, Ruth, and I recently had the privilege of attending a dinner at the Reagan Building in Washington, D.C., where we were among a group of parents being recognized for adopting children into our families. The delightful, beautiful actress Jane Seymour was among those being honored, and the event was hosted by Delilah, the well-known radio talk show host and best-selling author.

Delilah told us that a couple of years ago, she received an e-mail from a woman she had never met, suggesting that Delilah ought to go to Africa. At the time, Delilah had no plans to take a trip overseas, but the woman was persistent. Over the next several months, she sent several more messages, urging an African trip. Delilah finally decided that maybe God was trying to tell her something.

"So I went to Uganda, where I stayed in a village you couldn't imagine—without water, electricity, or anything else," she said.

Delilah was deeply moved by what she saw there—and especially by seeing hundreds of children who have lost their parents to AIDS. She was so touched by their plight, in fact, that she bought twenty-two hundred acres. "I want to build an orphanage there, where we can take care of as many of these kids as possible," she said.

Here is a woman who never imagined that she would travel to Africa, much less build an orphanage there. But she was willing to do whatever God wanted her to do, and hundreds of children will benefit as a result.

My friend Bobby Richardson, a standout second baseman

for the New York Yankees, is an outspoken Christian. When a reporter asked him if being a Christian made him a better ballplayer, Richardson responded, "Being a Christian makes me a better husband, a better father, and a better citizen . . . and that has to make me a better ballplayer."

Giving your life to Christ will change everything.

2. LIVING BY FAITH IS AN EXCITING ADVENTURE

The life I live in the body, I live by faith in the Son of God, who loved me and gave himself for me.
GALATIANS 2:20

A couple of months ago, I received an e-mail from an acquaintance who had been diagnosed with a brain tumor. Terrible news, to be sure.

But my friend's message wasn't full of fear and self-pity. She simply said she was trusting God, and she felt certain that He was going to heal her. But if He didn't choose to do that, whatever He had in mind for her was just fine.

Because of the brain tumor, the doctor ordered a full body scan, and it showed that she had a spot on her lung. It seemed likely that the brain tumor had metastasized.

But again, as she reported this to her friends and prayer partners, she was calm and trusting. She had an almost joyous anticipation of what God was about to do in her life.

At this point, I'll have to admit that I wasn't feeling too optimistic. If the cancer had spread, this was indeed a dangerous situation. But a few days later, I received another e-mail telling me that a pulmonary specialist had determined that the spot on her lung was not cancer at all but merely scar tissue left by a previous bout with bronchitis.

That was followed by more good news: further tests on the brain tumor showed that it was almost certainly benign, but the doctor still wanted her to see a surgeon because the tumor "had to come out."

She told him she was a Christian and wanted to delay a couple of weeks so she could pray about things. He gave her a look of sympathy. (He obviously didn't believe prayer was going to do much good, but he figured that he would at least humor her.) He agreed to her request for a delay.

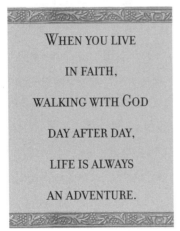

WHEN YOU LIVE

IN FAITH,

WALKING WITH GOD

DAY AFTER DAY,

LIFE IS ALWAYS

AN ADVENTURE.

When she went back in, two weeks later, the tumor was still there. But it was slightly smaller than before.

After thinking about it for a while, her doctor, who had at first been insistent that surgery was necessary, now said he didn't think the tumor posed any immediate danger. "Come back and see me in a year," he said, "and we'll take another look at the situation."

My friend was ecstatic, of course. She believes that when she goes in to see the doctor, the tumor will be gone. Whether or not that is the case, she will continue to trust God through it all and know that whatever He chooses for her is the best thing that could possibly happen. She also knows that when you live in faith, walking with God day after day, life is always an adventure.

Now, I don't want to make it sound like having faith means you won't get sick or have problems. But living by the faith phenomenon does mean that God will be with you in your time of testing. I want to make it clear that my friend does not know for certain that God will heal her. She does know, however, that He *could* heal her if that is His will for her, and she knows that her life is in His hands.

I have had other friends who were diagnosed with serious illnesses, who continued to trust God through difficult times, and who died. I have been devastated by such losses. My own father died in an automobile accident just two days after I graduated from Wake Forest University in 1962.

Faith does not mean you won't go through rough times. But it does mean that when hard times do come along, you can know that, as Billy Graham said, "God is sovereign even in things we don't understand." Pastor Rick Warren stated, "We find out that God is all we need when God is all we've got." We can also rest in the knowledge that, as my friend Jay Strack said, "God sees tomorrow like we see yesterday."

The Bible's eleventh chapter of Hebrews is known as "the faith chapter" because it talks about some of the miracles that happened because people were living by faith: "By faith the people passed through the Red Sea as on dry land. . . . By faith the walls of Jericho fell . . ." (verses 29–30).

Then this chronicle of faith abruptly switches gears:

> Others were tortured and refused to be released, so that they might gain a better resurrection. Some faced jeers and flogging, while still others were chained and put in prison. They were stoned; they were sawed in two; they were put to death by the sword. They went about in sheepskins and goatskins, destitute, persecuted and mistreated—the world was not worthy of them. They wandered in deserts and mountains, and in caves and holes in the ground. (verses 35–38)

Why do some suffer while others are blessed and rewarded? I have no idea. All I know is that God is in charge, and He can be trusted to do what is best for everyone concerned. And, as Paul said in Romans 8:18, "I consider that our present sufferings are not worth comparing with the glory that will be revealed in us."

No matter what happens here on earth, heaven is real. It waits for God's children. And it's better than anything you or I could possibly dream up.

Let me tell you about some other "adventures in faith" that have happened to friends of mine recently.

One friend told me that her pastor recently preached a series on the Ten Commandments, and she was especially convicted by his sermon about lying. She said she realized how often most people, even Christians, "fudge" on the truth, and she didn't want to do that anymore.

The very next week, she bought an elegant crystal bowl for a friend's birthday. As she was getting it out of her car, she dropped it and it cracked.

Of course, she was upset. When she told her friends about it, they all said, "Just take it back to the store and tell them it was cracked when you bought it." Even her Christian friends said, "Everybody does it."

"But I can't do that," my friend replied. "That would be lying . . . and I can't lie."

She loved the bowl, though, and wanted to get another one just like it. She went back to the store to get a replacement but couldn't find one on the shelf.

She told the store owner what had happened, and he went back into the stockroom to see if he could find another bowl just like the one she'd broken.

"You're in luck," he said as he came out carrying a box. "This is the last one."

He placed it on the counter, "There you go."

My friend pulled out her checkbook, but he said, "No charge. Just take it."

"But . . ." She started to protest that she knew it was expensive, and she was fully prepared to pay for it.

The store owner shook his head. "My gift to you," he smiled. "I appreciate your honesty."

How very much like God to do something like that! God is good—and He has a terrific sense of humor.

Another friend of mine was at Disney World with his wife and kids on a hot, humid summer day. His three children desperately wanted to go on the Jungle Cruise ride—but after

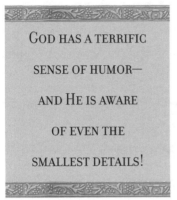

GOD HAS A TERRIFIC SENSE OF HUMOR— AND HE IS AWARE OF EVEN THE SMALLEST DETAILS!

about fifteen minutes of standing in the brutal heat, with the line barely moving, he started to pray silently, *God, please help us get on the Jungle Cruise ride.*

After a few minutes of this, he suddenly realized what he was doing. "Lord," he prayed, "please forgive me. There are children starving in this world, and people suffering from all kinds of terrible diseases . . . yet here I am praying to get on a ride at Disney World. I'm so sorry for my selfishness."

Then, in order to take a break and get out of the heat, he suggested, "Why don't we go get some ice cream?"

Everybody agreed that this was a good idea.

They got some chocolate-dipped cones and found a place in the shade to eat them. As they were enjoying their ice cream, my friend continued to pray silently, apologizing to God for his silly, selfish prayer.

But as soon as the ice cream was finished, one of the kids asked, "Can we go back to Jungle Cruise now?"

"But you saw what the line was like!" my friend protested.

"Please, Dad!"

The other kids chimed in, "Jungle Cruise! Jungle Cruise!"

Dad sighed. "Okay. I guess we can try."

When they got to the ride, my friend was surprised to see that there were *two* lines. One was completely full. The other was completely empty.

He and his wife looked at each other in surprise.

"Is that an entrance?" he asked.

"It looks like one to me!" she replied.

Less than a minute later, they were on board one of the jungle boats, floating past scary-looking crocodiles, hippos, and warriors on Disney's version of the Amazon.

You see, God has a terrific sense of humor—and He is aware of even the smallest details! Many millions of people can testify to the joy and excitement that comes from living a life of faith.

All those people can't be wrong. They can't be deceived. They can't be imagining things. They are living the exciting adventure of the faith phenomenon!

3. You Are Secure in God at All Times

The heavens are yours, and yours also the earth;
you founded the world and all that is in it.
PSALM 89:11

I know this world can be a dangerous and frightening place. We hear about terror alerts on the evening news. Our cities have become well acquainted with gang violence. There are wars and rumors of wars, wildfires, hurricanes, and killer floods. But through it all, champions feel secure, safe, and at peace because they are holding tightly to Christ's hand.

I recently came upon this passage from the first chapter of Nahum: "The LORD has His way in the whirlwind and in the storm, and the clouds are the dust of His feet" (Nahum 1:3 NKJV).

This verse had a particular significance to me, because Florida had just been battered by three hurricanes within the space of a month—Charley, Frances, and Ivan. As I pondered that verse from Nahum, I was reminded that God is always in control, that His power is present even in the hurricane, and that if our roots are anchored in Him, He will give us the power and grace to stand.

Hurricane Charley dealt a devastating blow to central Florida. Thousands of trees were toppled over, their roots lifted completely out of the ground. They were left scattered across the landscape like so many giant celery stalks.

As the storm cleanup continued, I received this e-mail from Amanda Ober, who is a reporter for Channel 2 in Orlando:

> After two weeks of reporting day after day on the aftermath of Hurricane Charley, God gave me a sweet and powerful insight I wanted to share. The vast majority of damage here in central Florida is from beautiful, grand trees known as water oaks that came crashing down on homes, businesses,

and lives. Did you know water oaks are notorious for having very shallow and weak root systems?

Throughout God's Word we are called to be sure our roots are planted deeply in Christ. When we worship Christ halfheartedly, giving Him only the leftovers of our time, our roots are shallow. Like the beautiful water oaks, we may appear grand and beautiful to all who cross our paths. We may have happy families, great jobs, and material blessings. But like the water oaks, because our roots are shallow, we will come crashing down when the storm hits. Our toppling will interrupt and even destroy not only our own lives, but the lives of those around us.

We will lose power for a period of time (think of all of us who suffered for so long with no electricity!), and we will be left with a mess that may take months to clean up, will cost us something, and will require the help of others.

She ends her message by paraphrasing Colossians 2:7: "Have your roots planted deep in Christ. Grow in Him. Get your strength from Him. Let Him make you strong in the faith as you have been taught. Your life should be full of thanks to Him."

Champions live as Paul urges: "Do not be anxious about anything, but in everything, by prayer and petition, with thanksgiving, present your requests to God. And the peace of God, which transcends all understanding, will guard your hearts and your minds in Christ Jesus" (Philippians 4:6–7).

Shortly after receiving Amanda Ober's e-mail, I was scheduled to fly to Atlanta for a speaking engagement. Airports were still closed due to the hurricane, so I drove from Orlando instead. The occasion was a fund-raiser to benefit abused and abandoned kids, and I wasn't about to miss it.

On the dais at the event, I found myself sitting next to a young Asian woman, who introduced herself to me as Kim Phuc. At first, the name didn't mean anything to me, but as she began to tell me about herself, I realized that I knew her story very well.

At the height of the Vietnam War, her village had been destroyed by a U.S. air strike. Kim, a little girl at the time, was photographed as she fled her burning village, screaming in terror and agony, horribly burned by napalm. Her photograph made the front page of newspapers all over the world. No one who has seen that dramatic, heartrending photograph will forget it.

I was thrilled beyond words to hear that Kim's life took a dramatic turn for the better after that horrible day. She became a Christian. She came to live in Toronto. She is happy and healthy, and the light of Christ's love shines in her eyes.

As I sat marveling at Kim Phuc's story, a choir of children from many nations came on stage and joined recording artist Amy Grant for a beautiful rendition of the song, "This Is My Father's World." On screens around the stage were projected beautiful slides of scenes from nature: a red leaf floating in a crystal-clear pond, a waterfall cascading down the side of a mountain, a meadow of brightly colored flowers, and so on.

As I looked and listened, I remembered the display of God's power I had just seen back home in Orlando, and tears came to my eyes. I am so grateful that this is my Father's world—even when the storms of life hit, as they will. Some ask why. I am happy to know that He holds the world—and all of His children, including you and me—in the palm of His hand. We are secure in Him at all times.

4. GOD WILL NEVER LEAVE YOU
Surely I am with you always, to the very end of the age.
MATTHEW 28:20

As I was writing this book, I received word that a longtime friend had died. His name was Don Shinnick, and he was an all-pro linebacker for the Colts for many years when they were in Baltimore. Don and I knew each other through our work with the Fellowship of Christian Athletes, and I can tell you that the world lost a great man with his passing.

Don was on the field for the Colts in the 1969 Super Bowl, when the New York Jets pulled off a shocking upset behind brash, young quarterback Joe Namath. Namath had guaranteed that his team would win the game, and then he backed up that statement by leading the Jets to a 16–7 victory.

As the teams left the field at the end of the game, Shinnick walked over and said something to Namath. Naturally, all the reporters wanted to know what Shinnick had said.

"I said, 'Don't forget the Lord,'" Shinnick told them.

Those are same words I want to say to you today.

Don't forget the Lord—no matter what happens in life. Don't get so caught up in your own success that you forget what He has done for you. Remember that He is with you at all times—whether you are on a high mountaintop or in a deep valley.

Never forget that you have this promise from God Himself: "I will never leave you nor forsake you" (Joshua 1:5). And, always remember, you can do anything through Christ! (see Philippians 4:13).

PUTTING IT ALL TOGETHER

*Success is peace of mind, which is a direct result of
self-satisfaction in knowing you did your best to
become the best that you are capable of becoming.*
JOHN R. WOODEN

We have come to the end of our "blueprint" for building a champion. I guarantee that if you put into practice the principles I've given you in this book, you will achieve success in life.

But you're the only one who knows for sure if you are a success. Nobody but you knows whether you are fully using the skills and talents God gave you. Only you know whether you feel fulfilled and content when you lie down in your bed at the end of the day. Nobody but you can tell whether your relationship with God is as it ought to be.

When Jesus had endured quite enough of the Pharisees, He told them they were a bunch of "whitewashed tombs" who looked good on the outside but who were full of death and decay inside (Matthew 23:27). That description applies to many people who live in our day. To the world, they look like the epitome of success. But when God looks at them, He sees past the makeup and the paint job, and He knows they are anything *but* successful.

That's why it's so important to remember what true success really is.

Before we say good-bye, I want to tell you four important things you need to know in order to hang on to your success—and to keep it in perspective so it doesn't give you a terminal case of big-headedness.

The four things you need to know are:

1. YOU HAVE TO KEEP COMPETING EVERY DAY.

2. REMEMBER THAT THE PAYOFF GOES TO THE WINNER.

3. CHAMPIONS ARE HUMBLE.

4. BE AWARE OF THE POWER OF YOUR INFLUENCE.

1. YOU HAVE TO KEEP COMPETING EVERY DAY

All athletes should bear in mind that they are competing, not with other athletes, but with their own capacities. Whatever I have already achieved, I have to go beyond, and I will.
CARL LEWIS

When I was in school, you couldn't do any better than a 4.0 grade point average. That was tops.

But at the last graduation I attended, there was a young man with a 4.0, and he wasn't even close to being the valedictorian or the salutatorian. The valedictorian had something like a 4.43 GPA. Don't ask me how you can get half a point higher than perfect straight As. I don't know.

But I do know this. Competition is fierce out there, and it's getting fiercer all the time. It is so important to keep yourself sharp and in condition to compete. You must keep learning, keep expanding your knowledge, keep refining your skills at all times.

Strive to be like Michelangelo, who, when he was eighty-four years old, and after all the great things he had done, said, "I am still learning." If you want to see just how important it is to keep competing, just take a look at the stock market, where yesterday's heroes quickly become today's zeroes, where yesterday's breakthrough technology is sometimes obsolete before tomorrow ever gets here. Stockholders are not all that interested in what you did last quarter. They want to know what you're doing right now.

Consider, too, an Olympic sport like the hundred-yard dash. Often, there's only a fraction of a second between the first- and last-place finishers. The difference is minuscule, but that little bit of speed makes all the difference.

Some people see competition as almost a dirty word. But it is far from that. Honest, healthy competition is a catalyst for growth in people, companies, communities, and societies. Competition pushes people forward. It propels them to invent new and better products.

Nobody understands better than I do that competition can be brutal. At the start of the 2003–2004 season, the Orlando Magic lost nineteen games in a row. The agony that everyone connected with a professional sports franchise goes through at a time like that is indescribable. All you can do is keep toughing it out, trying to improve, and learning from your mistakes. After losing those nineteen in a row, the Magic turned it around and won seven of ten, which was a great relief to those of us who were beginning to think we'd never win another game.

Still, I know that this rough spot in the road will benefit us and make us a better franchise in the long run. The same goes for you.

2. REMEMBER THAT THE PAYOFF GOES TO THE WINNER

Some guys think that coming to the park, suiting up,
and going out and playing is what you're getting
paid for. You get paid to suit up and win. There's
a big difference between those two approaches.
CURT SCHILLING

Some people just seem to know how to win. They may not be the people who get all the attention and glory. They may not be the guys who average twenty points a game or who hit thirty home runs every year. Sometimes they go almost unnoticed during the regular season. But then you look up during the playoffs, and there they are, playing an integral role for a championship team.

These guys have developed the habit of winning. They expect to win, and they do. I know it sounds simplistic, but it really is true that one of the most important keys to staying on top is believing you're going to win.

Winners have a number of other traits in common.

Winners are hard workers. Basketball great Larry Bird put it like this: "A winner is someone who recognizes his God-given talents, works his tail off to develop them into skills, and uses those skills to accomplish his goals."

Winners are forward looking. Bobby Knight, Texas Tech University basketball coach, has said that whenever his team wins a big game—or absorbs a discouraging loss—his immediate job is to get their minds off what just happened and get them to start focusing on and preparing for the next opponent. Too much time spent on today's victory or defeat will cause you to lose focus and could be disastrous in the weeks ahead.

Larry Bowa, former manager of the Philadelphia Phillies, had a plaque in his office that read, "Last year? History. Last night? In the books. Tonight? 110 percent!" Keep your mind on what you need to do now in order to be prepared when tomorrow comes.

Winners know the fundamentals. Winners are prepared in every situation. They are not guessing. They know what they're doing. George Allen, who had tremendous success as a football coach with the Washington Redskins and the Los Angeles Rams, was accurate when he said, "Winning can be defined as the science of being totally prepared."

Winners are unselfish. Here's what coach George Karl, who has had many years of success in the NBA, said: "As a team, you have to strangle the nature of selfishness. When you control it, you can be great, but when it raises its nasty demon head, it can kill you."

Winners know the importance of teamwork. The Boston Celtics' great center Bill Russell said, "I could have scored more, but it would have taken energy away from playing defense. We always won as a team, not individuals, and basketball is a team game. One man can't win it." And John Wooden said, "Ten strong horses could not pull an empty baby carriage if they worked independently of each other."

Never get to the point where you think you have it made—where you don't need to do anything more. Strive to be a winner in everything you do for the rest of your life.

In Major League Baseball, the guys who have long careers are generally the ones who work hard during spring training. They don't believe they can take it easy and coast through the preseason simply because they are veterans. They know there are talented younger players who would love to take their jobs away, and they stay on their toes to keep that from happening.

The principle applies to every other area of life. Champions don't rest on the reputation they earned yesterday. They are constantly showing that they have what it takes *today*!

3. CHAMPIONS ARE HUMBLE

He has showed you, O man, what is good.
And what does the LORD require of you?
To act justly and to love mercy
and to walk humbly with your God.
MICAH 6:8

The Bible has much to say about the importance of maintaining a humble attitude with God and our fellow man. Here are just a few of the relevant verses:

- "Whoever humbles himself like this child is the greatest in the kingdom of heaven." (Matthew 18:4)

- "Whoever exalts himself will be humbled, and whoever humbles himself will be exalted." (Matthew 23:12)

- "Do nothing out of selfish ambition or vain conceit, but in humility consider others better than yourselves." (Philippians 2:3)

- "Be completely humble and gentle; be patient, bearing with one another in love." (Ephesians 4:2)

People who are humble truly care about others. They don't think they are better than everyone else. They know that whatever they may have in life is a gift from God—that, when all is said and done, there is no such thing as a self-made man or woman.

After all, if you have a beautiful face, your beauty is a gift from God.

If people are always telling you that you have a wonderful singing voice, it was God who gave you that voice.

If you're an aspiring Major League pitcher with a 95-mph fastball, it was God who gave you the ability to throw the ball that fast.

If you have a degree from a top-notch business school and are rapidly climbing the corporate ladder, remember that it was God who gave you the brains to get your degree and then opened the doors for you to put that degree to work.

People who have a humble attitude genuinely care about other people. Perhaps you've heard the old saying, "People don't care what you know until they know you care." It may be a cliché, but like many other clichés, it's absolutely true.

Consider this: During the last few centuries, American churches have sent thousands of Christian missionaries to preach the gospel in Africa, Asia, and Latin America. Many left America with the attitude that said, "We have the truth, and we're going to convert the heathen." They went out with an attitude of arrogance and pride, as if the cultures they were going to couldn't possibly offer them anything of value in return.

Others went out with a humble attitude, with a loving desire to share Christ with those who had never heard of Him.

They had an attitude of humility, respect, and service—and a realization that they, too, would be learning and growing during their time in foreign cultures.

The message was the same in both instances—but the attitude was 180 degrees apart. It was arrogance versus humility. Over and over again, the humble attitude has proved to be the most effective means of sharing the good news of salvation through faith in Christ. It has left behind a strong, independent church, led by men and women from the indigenous culture.

You see, even if you're doing all the right things, if you're doing them for the wrong reason or with the wrong attitude, they won't matter very much. Remember what Paul said in 1 Corinthians 13:3: "If I give all I possess to the poor and surrender my body to the flames, but have not love, I gain nothing."

I heard about a group of teenagers from a church in an upper-middle-class suburb who went to a homeless shelter in the inner city to do some volunteer work. As they walked into the shelter, they passed a ragged, dirty wino sleeping it off on the sidewalk. The guy seemed to be out of it, so some of the kids made wisecracks about him and others talked about how disgusting he was.

Once they were safely inside the shelter, they were led into a conference room and told that the executive director would be joining them in a few moments. Imagine how surprised they were when, five minutes later, that disgusting "wino" walked through the door and announced that he was the one they were waiting for. He had only been pretending to sleep on the sidewalk, just to see how the teenagers would react to him.

When his guests were over their initial shock, he proceeded to explain to them how important it is to have a humble attitude toward others, to always treat people with kindness and respect. He explained, "If you really want to help people, you can't have a condescending attitude toward them."

I don't care what you may have accomplished in life. If you have lost your sense of humility, you don't have what it takes to be a champion.

4. BE AWARE OF THE POWER OF YOUR INFLUENCE

Here's a prayer I tried to live by as a manager: "Lord, when I'm wrong, make me willing to change. When I'm right, make me easy to live with. So strengthen me that the power of my example far exceeds the authority of my rank." I always tried to remember that you manage by influence and not authority.
ALVIN DARK

You may not think of yourself as a role model, but you are. Whether you know it or not, someone is watching you, comparing himself to you, and copying your behavior. The fact is that we are all role models. Everyone has a sphere of influence.

Most of us don't influence as many people as professional athletes and other celebrities do. But you might be surprised if you knew how many people are watching you, and even copying your behavior. Your sphere of influence may include your family, your friends, your neighbors, teammates, teachers, professors, and coworkers.

A champion not only says the right things, but he also strives to make sure that his actions line up with his words. He never wants to hear anyone say, "I can't hear your words because your actions are screaming so loudly."

I urge you to decide right now that you will strive to be a positive influence in every situation.

A Final Review

Let's go back now, one final time, and review the ten building blocks that will help you become the champion God always intended you to be:

1. Think the right kinds of thoughts.

Champions think thoughts that are positive, correct, big, pure, and unique. Every action begins as a thought, so make sure your thoughts are taking you in the direction you want to go.

2. Say the right kinds of words.

Champions know that the words they speak have tremendous power. Words can heal or hurt, build or tear down. Proper use of words will cause people to think of you as an intelligent, competent, caring person. But if you use words in the wrong context, are careless when it comes to grammar, or sprinkle your speech with slang, people who matter will tend to look down on you.

3. Set specific goals.

Write down your goals, make plans to achieve them, and work on your plans every single day. This advice, if you followed it, would be of more help to you than anything else you could ever learn. Setting goals and pursuing them takes persistence and self-discipline, but it is well worth the effort.

4. Take responsibility for your actions.

Champions don't whine about things they can't control. They don't look for someone or something to blame for their lack of success in life. Instead, they take responsibility for who they are and strive to do the best they can with the hand they've been dealt. They know that only about 10 percent of life is made up of what happens to you, and the other 90 percent has to do with what you do with what happens to you.

5. Choose the right kinds of friends.

The people with whom you surround yourself can help you succeed, or they can cause you to fail. That is why it is important to have friends who are able to bring out the best in you, who share your belief in God, and who are wise, loyal, and encouraging at all times.

6. Turn failures into strengths.

Champions understand that failure is an inevitable part of life for anyone who tries to do anything more than stay in bed with the covers pulled up over his or her head. Because they understand that failure is inevitable, champions do everything they can to learn and grow from their mistakes.

7. Go the extra mile.

Champions do more than is expected of them. They work harder on the job. They try harder in their relationships. They spend more time trying to develop their innate talents. They know that a person with a small amount of talent who works very hard will go much further than a person with a great deal of talent who isn't willing to make that extra effort.

8. Never give up.

Barbara Bush said of her son George W., "Whether you like him or not, he's tenacious." No matter what obstacles seem to be in their way, champions keep on putting one foot in front of the other, heading directly toward their goal. Walt Disney called this attitude "stick-to-it-ivity." Whatever you call it, every champion has it.

9. Remember that character counts.

Champions work on developing these character traits: commitment, honor, attitude, responsibility, abstinence, courage, truthfulness, ethics, and reputation.

10. Live by the faith phenomenon.

Accepting Christ as your Savior isn't where the adventure ends. That is just the beginning of the most amazing, incredible exciting life anyone could ever experience.

Baseball star J. D. Drew put it like this: "The plan of salvation is so simple, but so many people miss it because they think they can work their way to heaven. . . . The simplest thing to do is just ask God to forgive you and accept His Son, Jesus Christ, as your Savior and believe it with your heart."

Incorporate these ten building blocks into your life, and I guarantee that you will be a true champion.

We've come to the end of our journey now, and I want to leave you with these words from legendary champion Vince Lombardi: "After the cheers have died and the stadium is empty, after the headlines have been written, and after you are back in the quiet of your own room . . . and all the pomp and fanfare have faded, the enduring things that are left are: the dedication to excellence, the dedication to victory, and the dedication to doing with our lives the very best we can to make the world a better place in which to live."

I urge you to dedicate yourself to doing the very best you can to make yourself a better person and the world a better place to live. Cling to God's hand at all times. Do what you can to touch others with His love.

Do all this, and someday, when your life is over, you will hear these wonderful words from the Lord Christ Himself: "Well done, good and faithful servant! You have been faithful with a few things; I will put you in charge of many things. Come and share your master's happiness!" (Matthew 25:21).

Pat Williams is the senior vice president of the NBA's Orlando Magic, as well as one of America's top motivational, inspirational, and humorous speakers. Since 1968 Pat has been affiliated with NBA teams in Chicago, Atlanta, and Philadelphia, including the 1983 World Champion 76ers and now the Orlando Magic, which he co-founded in 1987 and helped lead to the NBA finals in 1995. Pat and his wife, Ruth, are the parents of nineteen children, including fourteen adopted from four nations, ranging in age from twenty to thirty-three.

You can contact Pat Williams at:
> Pat Williams
> c/o Orlando Magic
> 8701 Maitland Summit Boulevard • Orlando, FL 32810
> Phone (407) 916-2404 • pwilliams@orlandomagic.com
> Visit Pat Williams's Web site at: www.PatWilliamsMotivate.com

If you would like to set up a speaking engagement for Pat Williams, please write his business development manager, Andrew Herdliska, at the above address or call him at (407) 916-2401. Requests can also be emailed to aherdliska@orlandomagic.com or faxed to (407) 916-2986.

We would love to hear from you. Please send your comments about this book to Pat Williams at the above address or in care of our publisher at the address below. Thank you.

Denny Boultinghouse • Howard Books
3117 N. 7th Street • West Monroe, LA 71291
318-396-3122